Tales from Ancient China's Imperial Harem

Compiled by Yuan Yang and Xiao Yan
Translated by Sun Haichen

Foreign Languages Press   Beijing

First Edition 1998
Second Printing 2001

Home Page:
    http://www.flp.com.cn
E-mail Addresses:
    info@flp.com.cn
    sales@flp.com.cn

ISBN 7-119-02041-2
©Foreign Languages Press, Beijing, 1998, 2001

Published by Foreign Languages Press
24 Baiwanzhuang Road, Beijing 100037, China

Distributed by China International Book Trading Corporation
35 Chegongzhuang Xilu, Beijing 100044, China
P.O. Box 399, Beijing, China

Printed in the People's Republic of China

CONTENTS

INTRODUCTION

In ancient China the imperial harem, called the rear palace, was often astonishingly large. The common belief that it usually contained "three thousand beauties" or even more is borne out by historical records. In the period known as the Sixteen States (304-439), the ruler of the state of Zhao had no less than a hundred thousand lesser wives and woman attendants. Palace women in the Tang Dynasty (618-907) numbered over forty thousand. Emperor Shihuang of Qin, the first emperor in Chinese history, also had more than ten thousand women attending to his sensual desires.

The imperial harem of China underwent five phases in its development: (1) It was first set up in the Xia, Shang and Zhou dynasties (ca 21 century-221 B.C.). (2) It took form in the Qin and Han dynasties (221 B.C.-220), when a stratified system of imperial women with different titles and privileges was established. (3) It attained maturity in the Wei, Jin, Sui and Tang dynasties (220-960), when the structure of the imperial harem became basically fixed. (4) It underwent a period of consolidation in the Song, Yuan, Ming and Qing dynasties (960-1911). (5) It was dissolved after the founding of the Chinese Republic in 1911.

Throughout history numerous titles were bestowed on the imperial wives. In the Tang Dynasty, for instance, at least a hundred titles were given to the emperor's lesser wives. At the emperor's demise, his empress was elevated to the status of empress dowager and his consorts became the consorts dowager.

The emperor had full control over the destiny of his wives. Upon entering the palace as one of his wives, a woman had no choice but to try every means to win the favor of her imperial master. Her sole purpose was to give the emperor pleasure and

1

bear him heirs. More often than not, sorrow and grief became the dominant note of her life. Sometimes she managed to win the good graces of the emperor. Sometimes she was manipulated by powerful courtiers or eunuchs. In a few cases, she assisted the emperor in governing the country or reduced him to a puppet while wielding supreme power over the nation herself.

Thus some imperial women influenced the behavior of the Son of Heaven and even the policy of the imperial government. In various ways they helped shape the destiny of the dynasty. Thanks to their moral integrity and outstanding talents, some of them contributed to the benefits of the country and the people. There were also a few who, motivated by a vicious ambition, committed horrendous atrocities.

Depending on their family background and upbringing, the imperial women differed greatly in manners. Some indulged in wanton extravagance, and others were content to lead simple and honest lives.

Joy and sorrow went hand in hand in the imperial harem. Resplendent robes, pleasure excursions and sumptuous feasts were the order of the day. At the same time, a palace lady had many sorrows unknown to the country woman. She was separated forever from her family. With little chance to meet the emperor, she had to spend her days in loneliness and seclusion. Even if she was one of the lucky few to enjoy the emperor's favor, she still could have no sense of security and had to pit her wits against her rivals.

Most palace women were resigned to their hapless fate and died unfulfilled. Only a few wielded great power or even gained supremacy over the imperial court, sometimes at the expense of the country and the people.

The stories in this book, selected for their historical value or literary merit, vividly portray the social customs and palace life in ancient China and afford the readers new insights into the role of women in Chinese history.

LEIZU TEACHES PEOPLE TO SPIN SILK

The Chinese regard themselves as descendants of Huangdi (the Yellow Emperor) and Yandi (the Red Emperor), two legendary tribal kings who lived about 4,500 years ago.

As the story goes, when Huangdi was young he devoted himself so much to public welfare that he scarcely had the time to look for a wife. This made his parents a bit anxious. Eventually some elderly people visited his family with marriage proposals. Without exception the prospective brides were very pretty, much to the satisfaction of his parents. But Huangdi turned down all offers. "You have to be satisfied with one of these lovely maidens," his parents protested. Huangdi smiled. "I want my wife to be exceptional not in looks but in ability." His parents nodded their understanding and pressed him no more.

One day Huangdi was hunting in the west hill when he caught sight of a young woman under a big mulberry tree. She was kneeling on one knee, with one hand placed on the tree trunk. A lone thread of silk was coming out of her mouth and falling on the ground in a bundle the size of a jar. The silk produced by the young woman was first a golden color and then it turned to silver. From behind a rock Huangdi watched her, transfixed.

"I never expected to meet a silk-spitting girl!" Huangdi told himself. "Youcao taught people to build wooden houses, and Shennong taught them how to grow crops. People today no longer need to worry about food or shelter, but they still wear unsightly animal skins. How nice it would be to wear clothes made of silk!" He checked his impulse to call out to the girl and decided to wait until she finished.

3

After spinning three large cocoons, the girl stood up to leave. Huangdi stepped forward, bowing with clasped hands. "Please wait a minute, sister!"

Glancing at him, the girl asked, "What do you want, brother?"

"I wonder if you could teach me to make silk like you did a moment ago," he replied.

"My mother will allow me to teach only one person," said the girl.

"And who is that?"

"My future husband." The girl blushed, covering her face with both hands.

Her words quickened Huangdi's pulse, but his heart sank when he took a closer look at her. She was quite unattractive: short, dark-skinned, and thick-lipped. On second thought, Huangdi decided that it would be wonderful to have a silk-spitting girl for a wife. Plucking up courage, he said, "With your consent, I am ready to take you as my wife."

The girl walked up to him, and they sat down side by side on a rock. Huangdi then asked, "Now that we are engaged, can you tell me who you are and where you live?"

"My name is Leizu. I used to be a maid servant of the Heavenly Queen, who banished me to earth because of my transgression."

"What did you do?"

"One day I went to the garden with a few companions to enjoy the flowers there. A five-color plant, heavy with fruit, caught my eye. The fruit looked and smelled so inviting that I picked some and ate them. They tasted sweet. After I swallowed them, my stomach felt funny and I wanted to throw up. I crouched on the ground and began to spit silk.

"Just then some butterflies appeared from nowhere and started to circle the fragrant plant. I wondered if I could

5

make them spin silk also by feeding them the seeds of the plant. Well, after eating the seeds, the butterflies laid eggs, which turned into little worms. I fed these silkworms with the seeds, and they began to spit silk. I watched in fascination.

"Unfortunately a quick-tongued maid informed the Queen of what I had done. She flew into a rage and at once drove me out of Heaven. Thrown into a valley, I nearly fell victim to a pack of wolves. But an old woman named Xiling Shi happened to be gathering firewood there. She found me and took me to her home, so I acknowledged her as my mother. The two of us have lived together ever since."

Huangdi placed his hands on Leizu's shoulders, not knowing what to say. "I keep some silkworms on the northern slope of the hill," said Leizu. "They grow well by feeding on mulberry leaves. Some are spinning silk now. Let me take you there to look!"

Huangdi went with her and was pleased to find all the cocoons were as big as jugs. "I will return and send people over to fetch these cocoons," he said. Leizu smiled and nodded.

Back home, Huangdi told his parents that he had finally found himself a wife. The news spread quickly. When Huangdi brought Leizu to his house, he was greeted by a huge crowd. At the sight of the bride, however, someone whispered, "Why should he marry such a coarse girl when he has many pretty ones to choose from?" "Don't you worry," his companion responded. "Huangdi knows what he is doing. Maybe this girl is quite extraordinary." The sight of the cocoons also aroused great wonder among the spectators.

Leizu then began to demonstrate how to reel off raw silk from the cocoons and how to coil it up. Under her instruction, several girls followed suit. The sight of the fine silk coils brought happy smiles to the faces of everyone.

Leizu taught people to cultivate silkworms, spin silk and weave cloth. Thanks to Leizu, they began to wear clothes instead of animal skins. This gained her high esteem. The image of a god that used to be enshrined in the spinning room of every rural household was Leizu, Mother of Silk.

KING SHUN'S TWO WIVES, EHUANG AND NÜYING

In very ancient times the throne was not hereditary. A king was supposedly elected on the basis of his merits.

Like Huangdi, King Yao was also a renowned and sage ruler of ancient China. When he was old, people recommended Shun to be his successor. After testing Shun for a long time, Yao finally abdicated in his favor. He also married his two daughters to Shun.

Nüying, the younger one, was his natural daughter, but the elder one, Ehuang, was adopted. Yao doted on his daughters, who were both clever and attractive. He took them along on all his inspection tours across the country.

The two girls were only too happy to marry Shun, but Yao's wife had something else in mind. She wanted her birth daughter, Nüying, to be Shun's principal wife, with Ehuang only being his consort. Yao adamantly objected to such an arrangement. Instead, he suggested that the order of precedence be decided by the result of a three-part contest. The wife agreed reluctantly.

The first part of the contest was to cook some beans. Yao gave each daughter ten beans and five jin of firewood. Whoever cooked the beans first would be the winner.

As the elder daughter of the family, Ehuang had worked in the kitchen for many years. She poured a little water into a wok and had the beans done in a short time. Nüying, however, had no cooking experience. She filled the wok with water and used up all the firewood before the water was hot. Glumly Yao's wife had to admit that her favored daughter had lost the first round.

The second part of the contest was to stitch shoe soles.

Yao let his wife bring two strings of rope and a pair of cloth soles. Each daughter was then given a sole to stitch with the rope. Whoever finished first would be the winner.

With plenty of experience, Ehuang knew exactly what to do. She cut the rope into short pieces, using them one by one. In less than half a day, the sole in her hands was well sewn with close stitches. Not knowing how to do this, Nüying tried to sew with the long rope, which often became quite knotted as she worked. In half a day her work was not yet half done, and the stitches already sewn were quite irregular. Annoyed, Yao's wife decided to try to find a way to save the situation.

When the appointed wedding day drew near, Yao announced the third part of the contest. His two daughters would leave for Lishan, where Shun lived, at the same time, and whoever arrived first would be the winner.

At this Yao's wife remarked, "Because she is the elder sister, Ehuang should ride in a carriage, and only a three-horse carriage is fit for this great occasion. The younger sister, Nüying, can make do with a mule." Though aware of his wife's partiality, Yao did not object.

Taking a shortcut, Nüying sped along on the mule. Ehuang, on the other hand, rode in the carriage at a leisurely pace. But half way there, Nüying's mule suddenly gave birth. "What a vicious animal to spoil everything for me like this!" she cursed angrily. "From now on the mule must never give birth again!" As is widely known, her curse has been fulfilled. The place was later named Luoju (Foal Birth) Village.

Ehuang meanwhile arrived at the scene in her carriage and picked up her distressed younger sister. Together they rode to Lishan.

Shun treated Ehuang and Nüying with no partiality, and made no distinction of status between them. With their devotion and support, he ruled the country with great benevolence and fulfilled many tasks that benefitted of his people. During his reign he made frequent inspection tours to make sure that the people were living in peace and contentment.

At a hundred years of age he made one more tour to the south, although by that time he had already abdicated the throne in favor of Yu. Seized by a sudden illness, he died at Cangwu Mountain (modern Ningda County in Hunan Province). The news threw the entire nation into deep grief. Ehuang and Nüying, who had shared weal and woe with him for dozens of years, wept uncontrollably. Hastening to the south, they passed a bamboo forest where they wept so bitterly that the bamboo trunks were left with indelible tearstains. This was how the tearstain variety of bamboo came into existence in south China.

Yu was also grieved by the death of his predecessor. Accompanied by his ministers, he went to the Cangwu Mountain to hold a grand funeral for Shun. To commemorate the great ruler he had a mausoleum and a temple built there. The two constructions survive to this day.

After the funeral Yu returned north, taking Ehuang and Nüying with him. The two sisters, heartbroken over the death of their husband, drowned themselves in the Xiang River. They are said to have turned into immortals, known as the Xiang goddesses. Thus tearstain bamboo is now called Xiang Goddess bamboo.

NÜJIAO ENCOURAGES HER HUSBAND TO TAME FLOODS

In ancient times floods were a common calamity. During Shun's reign, about four thousand years ago, a flood-fighting hero called the Great Yu emerged. Yu's father, Gun, had tried for nine years to tame the floods at Shun's order, but to no avail. Because of his failure, he was executed by Shun at Yushan.

Fully occupied in his flood control mission, Yu remained single until he was more than thirty years old. At Tushan he met Tushan Shi's daughter, Nüjiao, who was a renowned beauty. They fell in love at once. When Yu was called away by his duty, Nüjiao missed him dearly and composed a song to describe the anguish of her longing. Yu was greatly moved when Nüjiao's maid told him about it. They finally got married at a place called Taisang.

Four days after the wedding Yu bade his wife good-bye and left to fight the floods away from home. During the next thirteen years he passed his house three times without entering. Then one morning, about four years after his departure, he came home for the first time. On approaching the gate, he overheard his mother grumbling, "The father tried to tame the flood and met his death at Yushan. The son also tried to tame the flood and disappeared for four years. The father was a simpleton and the son is an imbecile!"

Just then a child burst out crying and was scolded by Yu's mother. "Will you ever stop crying? If you must cry, go and cry to your father. That would save your grandmother a lot of trouble!" This was followed by Nüjiao's voice comforting the

child.

The old woman grew more vindictive. "The husband left four days after wedding and stayed away for four years. The wife is a bride in name and a widow in fact!" Nüjiao sighed deeply but said nothing.

Yu checked his impulse to enter the house. What could he say to his mother's bickering? He had a mission to fulfill, and there was no time to lose. So he left without entering to say hello to his family.

About three years later Yu came home again at midday. Overcome with homesickness the night before, he had set out on horseback before dawn, coming to the mound by his house at noon. He saw kitchen smoke rising from the chimney and heard a long cockcrow and the grunting noise from the pigsty. Everything seemed to be in order, he thought to himself.

Just then he heard his mother's hearty laughter. "My grandson, what would you do if your father came home and didn't recognize you?"

"If he doesn't recognize me, I'll smite him!"

"Why?" It was the voice of Nüjiao.

"Why not, if he can't even recognize his own son?" The child squealed. "He would deserve it!"

"Good boy," Yu's mother said. "You certainly take after me!" This was followed by another fit of laughter.

"Last time I heard whining, weeping and sighing," Yu thought to himself, "and yet I didn't enter the house. This time I hear joy and laughter, so there is still less need for me to enter." He left again for the flooded area.

One day about three or four years later, his work took Yu to a place near his home. At noon dark clouds gathered in the sky, followed by a torrential rain. In spite of the bad weather Yu set out on horseback and arrived home at dusk. How nice it would be to take a rest, meet his family, dry his clothes over the fire, and enjoy a meal in warmth and comfort!

Heading straight for the gate of his house, he caught sight

13

of a boy trying to drain rainwater from the eaves. The boy looked up and greeted him in a high-pitched voice. "Hey, Uncle, have you even seen my dad?"

"Who is your dad?"

"He is the Great Yu! If you see him, uncle, please tell him to come home and help me dig a ditch in front of the house."

Just then Yu heard his mother's voice inside the house. "Stop talking nonsense, you little devil! Your father is responsible for fighting floods all over the country. He is just beginning to make a bit of success, and you want him back to dig a ditch for you?"

Then it was Nüjiao's voice. "Your grandmother is right. Dad won't come home until he has tamed all the floods under heaven."

Yu was greatly pleased. "All right," he said to his son. "I promise to pass on your message to him."

With this he mounted his horse and galloped off.

It took Yu thirteen years of the most arduous efforts to tame all the floods in the country. People in the flooded areas could then rebuild their homes. When Yu finally returned home, his son was a teenage boy, and his wife a middle-aged woman.

Because of his merits in taming the floods, Yu won high esteem among the people and succeeded Shun in ruling the nation. He became King Yu, and Nüjiao became the queen. Today, Yu is remembered as one of China's sagest rulers, and Nüjiao as a great woman who made willing sacrifices for the benefit of the people.

WU JIANG, A PARTIAL MOTHER

The Eastern Zhou Dynasty, subdivided into the Spring and Autumn Period and the Warring States Period, was a time of constant contention and strife among vassal states.

During the reign of King Ping of Zhou (770-719 B.C.), Duke Wu of the state of Zheng distinguished himself among the vassal lords by his numerous exploits.

Duke Wu had two sons by his wife, Wu Jiang. When giving birth to Wusheng, the eldest son, Wu Jiang nearly died in labor, and so she disliked him strongly. The younger son, Duan, was a handsome, sweet-tongued lad skilled in martial arts. Wu Jiang often spoke to her husband in Duan's favor, trying to persuade him to make the younger son his heir. Duke Wu, however, did not give his assent.

After Duke Wu's death Wusheng ruled Zheng as Duke Zhuang. Like his father, he was appointed by the King of Zhou to be a minister in the royal court. As Duan had no share in the honors and privileges enjoyed by his elder brother, Wu Jiang went to complain to Duke Zhuang. "You have succeeded your father as the Duke of Zheng, but your brother still has no place of his own. I can't have him stay by my side forever."

"What do you think should be done, mother?" asked Duke Zhuang.

"Can you give him the fiefdom of Zhiyi?"

"Zhiyi is the most important city in Zheng next to the capital. My late father made it clear that no one was to have Zhiyi as his fief."

"Well then, Jingcheng will also do."

When Duke Zhuang did not reply at once, Wu Jiang got exasperated. "All right, no place is fit to be his fief. Why don't you just banish your brother and let him starve to death?"

Duke Zhuang hastily apologized. "Don't be angry with me, mother. I'll give this matter due consideration."

The next day, when Duke Zhuang disclosed to his ministers his intention to enfeoff Duan at Jingcheng, they raised vigorous objections. "It is out of the question!" cried one of them. "Jingcheng is a big city no less important than the capital, Xingyang. What's more, the duchess dowager has a strong partiality for Duan. If we let him settle in Jingcheng and build it into his power base, it would probably mean big trouble for our state."

"My mother wants it this way," Duke Zhuang rejoined. "How can a son disobey his mother?" Ignoring protests from his ministers, Duke Zhuang gave his brother the fiefdom of Jingcheng.

Before his departure, Duan went to bid his mother farewell. She took him by the hand and stroked his arm gently. "I'm leaving, Mother," said Duan. "Don't worry about me."

"There is no need to hurry!" Wu Jiang said. "I have something to tell you." In a hushed voice, she went on, "Your brother has no sense of kinship. Though he agreed to give Jingcheng to you upon my insistence, in his heart he was really unwilling to do so. When you arrive there, don't idle away your time. You have to plan for your future. Expand the troops under your command, drill them regularly, and store plenty of food and provisions. Once the opportunity comes, I will give you a message. On receiving it you must set out at once with your troops to attack the capital, and I will try to lend you a hand from inside. Zheng will surely fall into your hands. With you set up as the Duke of Zheng, I will die with a contented heart!"

All went well for Duan in Jingcheng. Bearing his mother's words in mind, he kept expanding his forces and giving them rigorous training. When news of this activity reached the capital, several ministers advised Duke Zhuang to do something to discipline his younger brother, but the duke rebuked them for being impertinent. "He makes all these efforts in order to defend our state better," the duke declared. Many ministers grew worried that the duke, by letting Duan loose on his fief, was feeding a tiger to his own detriment.

Shortly after, Duan attacked and occupied two small towns adjacent to Jingcheng. The magistrates of the two towns fled to the capital and told Duke Zhuang how Duan had taken over their towns by force. Duke Zhuang merely nodded, saying nothing. Many ministers then became agitated. "Duan is constantly expanding his troops, and now he has occupied two towns. He is undoubtedly raising a revolt. We must send an expedition at once!" Hearing this, Duke Zhuang frowned and reproached them for being unreasonable. "Duan is my mother's favorite," he said. "I would rather lose a few cities than hurt my mother's feelings by taking any action against my brother."

"If you let Duan have his will, someday he may go against your will," said General Lü. "What will we do then?"

"We need not discuss this any longer," Duke Zhuang declared. "When that day comes, people will not doubt who is in the right."

Some days later Duke Zhuang went to Luoyang, the royal capital, to execute his duties to the King of Zhou. He entrusted the state affairs to the care of his most trusted ministers, for he was to be away for quite some time. At the news of Duke Zhuang's departure, Wu Jiang immediately wrote a letter to Duan and had it taken to Jingcheng by a trusted servant. In the letter, she told him to fix a date on which to attack the capital, and she told him that she promised to take concerted action from within.

Upon receiving the letter, Duan wrote back at once. Then he gathered his troops and told them, "The Duke has invited me to return to the court on urgent business." Thus they set out for the capital without delay.

Duke Zhuang, however, did not leave for the royal capital. Instead, he led two hundred war chariots to Jingcheng by a roundabout route. He stopped the troops near Jingcheng and waited for Duan to leave. At his order General Lü sent some men to lie in ambush by the road. They caught Duan's messenger and brought him back. Duan's letter to Wu Jiang was discovered.

Some of General Lü's men, disguised as merchants, then entered Jingcheng. After Duan left the city, they set the gate tower on fire. At this signal Duke Zhuang and General Lü led their troops into the city.

Two days after his departure, Duan was informed of the loss of Jingcheng. He led the troops on a forced march overnight to return to his fief, hoping to recapture it. But after his intention to rebel against Duke Zhuang became known, half of his soldiers deserted. Knowing he could not return to Jingcheng, Duan went to Yancheng, where he lost a battle to the duke. He then fled to another small city. Duke Zhuang and General Lü quickly closed in and laid siege to that city.

Unable to withstand such a vigorous attack, the city soon succumbed. "My mother has led me to death!" Duan cried before he committed suicide. When Duke Zhuang arrived at the scene, he burst into tears holding his brother's body in his arms. "O Brother, why did you do this? Wouldn't I forgive you for whatever you did?" The utter grief displayed by the duke moved many of the onlookers to tears.

A search of Duan's body uncovered his mother's letter. In a rage Duke Zhuang ordered that both letters taken to his mother back in Xingyang. Then he exiled her to Chengying, a small city near the capital, with the pledge, "We shall never meet until both of us are under the ground!"

A few days later Duke Zhuang returned to the capital. Gradually, he began to grow uneasy about his mother's absence. He had always wanted to be a filial son. However, he had sworn never to meet her until they were under the ground and did not want to arouse the gods' wrath or lose his people's trust by going back on his word.

Just then Ying Kaoshu, an official from Chengying, came to call on Duke Zhuang. He offered the duke some venison together with a strange-looking bird. "What bird is this?" asked the duke. "This evil bird is called an owl," replied Ying Kaoshu. "It sees nothing during the day but sees everything at night. It confuses black with white and confounds right with wrong. Fed by its mother when small, it eats its mother when it grows up. I have brought this bird to you, my lord, so you can punish it properly." The duke realized what Ying Kaoshu was driving at, but made no comment.

It was already noon, so Duke Zhuang invited Ying Kaoshu to lunch. At the table the duke placed some meat on Ying's plate. Ying Kaoshu picked out the best piece and wrapped it up. Upon the duke's inquiry, he explained, "My family is not well-to-do, and there is seldom a meat dish on the table. Unless I can bring some meat back to my aged mother, I will not be able to enjoy such a feast."

Duke Zhuang heaved a deep sigh. "You are without a doubt a filial son. Though I am your lord, I cannot pay respects to my mother like you do."

"Is there anything wrong?" asked Ying Kaoshu deliberately.

With another deep sigh, Duke Zhuang recounted the cause of the discord between himself and his mother.

"Don't worry, my lord," said Ying Kaoshu. "While you are thinking of your mother, she must be thinking of you! A person doesn't have to die to go underground. We can dig a tunnel, build an underground house, and fetch your mother to live there. Then you can go down into the tunnel to visit her."

Duke Zhuang was delighted with this way to make up with his mother without breaking his word. He put Ying Kaoshu in charge of the project. Having five hundred men under his command, Ying Kaoshu quickly dug the tunnel and built the underground house. Wu Jiang was taken to the house, and Duke Zhuang went there to visit her. Falling on his knees, he said, "Mother, please forgive your unfilial son," and cried like a child.

Feeling sad and a bit ashamed, Wu Jiang pulled the duke to his feet. "It was all my fault. Why should you be blamed!"

The mother and son embraced and wept together. Duke Zhuang took his mother by the hand and led her out of the tunnel. They mounted a carriage and rode along several main streets in the capital before finally returning to the palace.

The people of Zheng were favorably impressed. "What a filial son our lord is!" they exclaimed in wonder.

Duke Zhuang was grateful to Ying Kaoshu for his brilliant idea. Moreover, he found Ying to be a talented and widely respected official. Thereupon Ying Kaoshu was promoted to be a minister of the court.

LI JI MURDERS
THE CROWN PRINCE

Duke Xian of Jin (770-475 B.C.) and his wife, Qi Jiang, had a son and a daughter. The son, Shen Sheng, was made crown prince. After his wife's death, Duke Xian married two women from the Di family. Each gave birth to a son. The elder one was Chong Er, and the younger one, Yi Wu. Later, Duke Xian defeated a tribe called Lirong. To sue for peace, the tribe offered Duke Xian a beauty named Li Ji together with her younger sister. Duke Xian had two more sons, Xi Qi and Zhuo Zi, by Li Ji and her younger sister.

Thus the duke had five sons by his five wives. Predictably, they fought fiercely for his attention and favor.

In addition to her good looks Li Ji excelled in the gift of pleasing her husband. Thus, among his five wives Duke Xian liked her the best. He even intended to make her son his heir. The problem was that he had set up Shen Sheng as the crown prince before he married Li Ji.

When Duke Xian first mentioned his intention to Li Ji, she had a hard time concealing her exultation. Falling on her knees, she said in a serious tone, "You have already made Shen Sheng the crown prince, and the fact is known among the vassal lords. In addition, the crown prince has proved himself to be very capable. How can you depose him for my sake? As the sovereign, you should act in the best interest of our nation." Duke Xian put the matter aside, impressed by Li Ji's unselfishness.

In the meantime Li Ji quietly set out to replace Shen Sheng with her own son. She wanted to achieve that goal in such a way that it would not arouse people's suspicion.

There were two sycophantic courtiers, Liang Wu and

Dong Guanwu, who had a great influence on the duke and held sway over the court. Li Ji had a trusted follower named Shi, a handsome court performer with winning ways. For her sake, the duke also bestowed much favor on him.

Li Ji sent Shi to bribe Liang Wu and Dong Guanwu, who then agreed to assist her in her plot. At their advice, she found excuses to have Shen Sheng sent to Quwo, and two other sons, Chong Er and Yi Wu, sent to Pudi and Qudi, thereby getting them out of her way. As for the court ministers who did not sympathize with her, her strategy was to send them to accompany Chong Er and Yi Wu, on the pretext that the two young princes needed able advisors. In order to boost the esteem of her own son, Xi Qi, she invited Duke Xian's most trusted minister, Xun Xi, to tutor him.

Gradually Duke Xian lost almost all contact with Shen Sheng and his ministers. Only Li Ji and her adherents had the opportunity to converse regularly with the duke. While Xun Xi kept praising Xi Qi for his intelligence, Liang Wu and Dong Guanwu spoke ill of Shen Sheng almost every day.

At this juncture the state of Jin suffered an invasion by horsemen from a northern tribe. Li Ji called Liang Wu and Dong Guanwu to her. "You can certainly persuade the duke to send Shen Sheng to repulse the northern horsemen. With all the troops under your command, you can select a band of old and weak soldiers for him. Even if he should escape death on the battlefield, he will surely be executed for his defeat."

Duke Xian, suspecting nothing, sent Shen Sheng on the expedition. But much to Li Ji's disappointment, the invading army was so small that Shen Sheng had little difficulty chasing them back across the border. Li Ji thus had to develop another plot to get rid of Shen Sheng.

One day Li Ji said to the duke, "You are getting on in years, my lord, and you need a son to assist you in holding court. My son, Xi Qi, is too young. Why don't you call back the crown prince? Don't you miss him after he has been away for so many years?" Duke Xian accepted her advice and sent a messenger to Quwo to fetch Shen Sheng.

On his return Shen Sheng went straight to the palace to see his father and Li Ji. After he bade farewell to the duke, Li Ji invited him to her residence where a banquet was held to welcome his return. When he had drunk a few cups of wine, Li Ji began a genial conversation, inquiring after his life away from the capital. As he rose to leave, she said, "The flowers are in full bloom in the rear garden. You have been working hard all these years. Why not take a rest tomorrow and accompany me on a tour of the garden? I can also do with some rest and relaxation." Shen Sheng readily agreed.

That evening Duke Xian was drifting into sleep when Li Ji began to sob. Upset, the duke sat up in bed and asked gently, "Come on, my love, don't cry like this. If you have any grievance, don't hesitate to tell me." Li Ji's tears flowed more profusely. "What on earth has happened?" asked the duke anxiously. "Tell me who has offended you and I'll punish him at once."

Li Ji moved her lips as if to speak, but no words came. Then, as Duke Xian became impatient, she finally muttered, "It is the crown prince. He ... he made passes at me. I tried to ignore him. When he stepped forward to embrace me, I hastily pushed him away. But he would not give up and invited me to tour the rear garden with him tomorrow."

"How could this happen?" the duke mumbled angrily. "How dare he?"

Li Ji mistook the duke's rage for disbelief, so she wept on bitterly. "I didn't want to tell you," she sobbed. "I knew you wouldn't believe me. But what can I do from now on? If you watch from a distance when he meets me in the garden tomorrow, you'll see how impertinent he is."

At the center of the rear garden was a big flower bed surrounded by rockeries of various shapes, with a crystal clear stream flowing underneath. In the north stood a tower overlooking the entire garden. It was there that Duke Xian decided to conceal himself to find out the truth.

The following day Li Ji got up early and put on her make-up carefully. She was fond of wearing flowers in her hair, and on this day for the first time she smeared the flowers with honey.

When Shen Sheng arrived, Li Ji received him very cordially and showed him around the garden, pointing out and naming the exotic flowers for him. Then she led him toward the north, where she knew the duke was intently watching from the tower.

Arriving under the tower, Li Ji walked directly into the cluster of flowers and some bees, attracted by the honey, began to circle her head. In a frightened voice she whispered to Shen Sheng, "Look, these bees are so annoying! They just won't leave me alone! Can you chase them away for me?" Shen Sheng raised his broad sleeve to chase the bees. "No, they are over here!" cried Li Ji. Shen Sheng raised the other arm. From a distance it looked as if he were trying to embrace her.

Duke Xian had been seething with rage ever since he first saw Shen Sheng and Li Ji walking side by side. Shen Sheng's seeming attempts to hug her pushed him over the edge. Bristling in wild fury, he staggered down from the tower.

Li Ji saw the duke coming and whispered to Shen Sheng, "The world is turning around!". "Give me a hand!" As she said this, she acted as if she were about to faint. No sooner had Shen Sheng placed his hand on her waist to steady her than she cried out, "You ... get away from me!" Giving him a heavy push, she nearly sent him sprawling.

Duke Xian arrived in time to witness the scene. Unable to contain his fury, he wanted to have Shen Sheng put to death immediately. Wiping off her tears, Li Ji pleaded with him, "The crown prince was rude indeed, but to execute him on account of this would not seem justified. Some people would blame you for failing to discipline your eldest son; some would even accuse me of trying to implicate him. Please spare him this time." Duke Xian, struck by her kindness and generosity, agreed. He found an excuse to send Shen Sheng back to Quwo.

Though deeply perplexed, Shen Sheng did not suspect that Li Ji was trying to persecute him. Back in Quwo, he quickly forgot the incident.

Some days later Li Ji sent a message to Shen Sheng, saying, "The day after tomorrow will be the anniversary of your mother's demise. When you offer a sacrifice on that day, do everything in accordance with the rites." Shen Sheng was impressed by Li Ji's solicitude. When the day came, he conducted the sacrificial ceremony with due formalities. Afterward he had a portion of sacrificial meat sent to every family member, relative, and friend. When a piece of meat was brought to the palace, Li Ji received it because Duke Xian was away on a hunting excursion.

On his return from the hunting trip Duke Xian felt hungry and tired. "The crown prince offered a sacrifice to his mother today," Li Ji told him, "and he has sent us some wine and meat."

The hungry duke immediately picked up a slice of the meat from the table, but Li Ji stopped him, saying, "We must be careful when we eat any food from outside the palace. Let me test it first." She had a dog brought in and threw the slice of meat to it. After eating the meat, the dog rolled on the ground and died almost instantly. "I can't believe this!" exclaimed Li Ji. "I wonder if the wine is poisoned too?" She called in a palace maid and ordered her to taste the wine. The maid was also poisoned to death immediately.

"I did not know the crown prince could be so vicious!" Li Ji cried in utter grief. "I forgave him for being indecent to me, but how dare he plot against you in return!" The duke, shaking with uncontrollable rage, was unable to say a word. "Maybe you shouldn't blame him," Li Ji went on, as if trying

25

to comfort the duke. "Perhaps the crown prince did not intend to harm you. When he took liberties with me in the garden, I pushed him away very forcefully. That must have offended him a great deal, so he probably wants to get even with me. I might as well eat the meat. With me dead, the palace will be at peace, and the crown prince will be appeased." With tears streaming down her cheeks, she picked up a slice of the poisoned meat.

Duke Xian felt a stab in his heart at the sight of Li Ji's grief-stricken face. He took her into his arms. "My beloved, please don't! I wanted to execute that beast before, and it was you who persuaded me to spare him. This time I will definitely have no mercy on him! Don't try to stop me again!" Li Ji seemed too absorbed in weeping to say anything.

Duke Xian left in a huff and summoned his ministers for an emergency meeting. "Shen Sheng attempted to murder his father! He must be put to death for such a heinous deed!" With all the honest and upright officials ousted from power long ago, none of the ministers present raised any objections. Duke Xian sent Dong Guanwu and Liang Wu at the head of two hundred war chariots to seize Shen Sheng.

A sympathetic old minister sent a man to travel posthaste to Quwo with the news. Shen Sheng asked his tutor, Du Yuankuan, what to do. "The case is crystal clear," Du replied. "The sacrificial meat must have been poisoned by someone in the palace. It took a long time for the meat to be transported from Quwo to the capital, and then it was kept in the palace for a while before the duke returned from hunting. If it had been poisoned here, the meat would surely have changed color by the time it was placed on the table for the duke. You only have to present this argument to the duke to clear yourself of the trumped-up charge."

Shen Sheng, however, intended to fulfill what he considered the duties of a filial son and loyal subject. "When my father and sovereign wants me to die, I would be disloyal if I didn't."

"As your tutor I dare not induce you to be disloyal," Du said. "I just want to save you from dying without cause, and leaving a tainted name to posterity."

Shen Sheng refused to listen. "My father is very old, and Li Ji is the joy of his life. Without her he would not be able to eat or sleep. Even if I could clear myself of the charge, my father would be deeply hurt. Let my death wash away everything."

Du Yuankuan suggested, as a last resort, that the prince take refuge in a neighboring state until his father's wrath subsided. "No lord would want me on his territory," said Shen Sheng, "when it becomes known that I tried to murder my own father. My life has come to its end." Weeping bitterly, he went into his room and committed suicide.

At the news of the crown prince's death Chong Er and Yi Wu realized that it might be their turn next. They fled the state of Jin in a hurry.

With the crown prince dead and the other two brothers in exile, Xi Qi was erected as the heir apparent, much to Li Ji's satisfaction. Soon after, Duke Xian fell ill. On his deathbed he entrusted Xi Qi and Zhuo Zi to the care of Minister Xun Xi. At Duke Xian's death, Xi Qi, then only eleven years old, was made ruler of Jin. However, he was assassinated at Duke Xian's funeral by two ministers, Li Ke and Pi Zheng. When Xun Xi erected Zhuo Zi as the new duke, Li Ke murdered them both. With no one to rely on, Li Ji sank into despair and drowned herself. A nation without a sovereign, the state of Jin thereafter entered a chaotic period.

XI SHI, THE BEAUTY
WHO TOPPLES A NATION

In the fifth century B.C. China was at the end of the Spring and Autumn Period. The southern states of Wu and Yue were constantly at war. Wu finally conquered Yue and imprisoned its king, Gou Jian, for three years. After suffering numerous insults, Gou Jian returned to Yue and vowed to take revenge. To remind himself of the national humiliation, he had the soft mattress on his bed replaced with a layer of brushwood. Before each meal he tasted bitter herbs hanging by the table to recollect the bitterness of defeat. By enduring all these self-imposed hardships he strengthened his resolve to seek vengeance.

Gou Jian had a capable minister named Wen Zhong, who devised seven strategies for defeating Wu: 1. Offer handsome bribes to the Wu court to keep the King of Wu and his ministers happy and off guard; 2. Purchase plenty of grain from Wu to deplete its food reserve; 3. Present the King of Wu with beautiful maidens to divert his attention from state affairs; 4. Send high-quality bricks, tiles and timber along with skilled carpenters and bricklayers to Wu, inducing it to drain its manpower and resources in gigantic construction projects; 5. Dispatch spies to infiltrate into the Wu court; 6. Spread rumors in Wu to estrange the loyal and upright ministers from their king; and, 7. Store food and provisions and build up a strong army. Acting on Wen Zhong's advice, Gou Jian finally succeeded in wiping out the state of Wu. In this process a crucial role was played by Xi Shi, the beauty he sent to bewitch the King of Wu.

The Yarn-Washing Girl at the Foot of Zhuluo Hill

Zhuluo Village at the foot of Zhuluo Hill in the state of Yue was divided into the east and west sections by a small river running down from a hill. In west village there lived a young girl named Xi Shi, whose best friend was Zheng Dan, a neighbor's daughter. Both were good at cultivating silkworms and weaving cotton and silk, and they often went together to the river to wash clothes. Xi Shi was not only beautiful but she was also lively, clever, and nimble-handed. Nourished by the green hills and clear waters, she grew into a stunning beauty, her skin pure and soft like jade, her waist supple and slender like a willow twig in spring, her long, glossy black hair cascading down her shoulders, and her eyes gleaming tenderness and affection. Though she wore no make-up or adornments, her charms were captivating and irresistible. Young people in the area were all enamored of her, and her matchless beauty became known far and wide. Compared with Xi Shi, Zheng Dan was more willowy and lacked suppleness in her stature, but she was also considered a rare beauty with unique appeals.

The news that the King of Yue would select some beautiful maidens to be presented to the King of Wu came as a shock to the entire village. When officers from the county arrived at Zhuluo Village, they put both Xi Shi and Zheng Dan on their list. The two families and the rest of the villagers had to guarantee the safety of the two girls. If they should run away or commit suicide to avoid being sent to the King of Wu, the entire village would be held responsible.

Xi Shi lived with her father, who was sick, and Zheng Dan with her mother, who was blind. The two old people were sure they could not continue to live if their daughters were taken away from them, so they went together to plead with the officers. "Once our daughters are sent away to Wu, they'll never come back! How can we live on without them?"

"If they are chosen for the task, the King will pay you accordingly."

"What would be the use of that? We would be deprived of the light of our day! Why should our King use such an ignoble method to fight the enemy? Can't he find a better way? Why doesn't he marry his own daughter to the King of Wu? Doesn't he feel ashamed of what he is doing to us?"

Swearing at the two old people, the officers had Xi Shi and Zheng Dan placed into a carriage. They left the village for the capital escorted by armed guards.

Xi Shi and Zheng Dan excelled among the beauties gathered in the capital. Together with a few others, they were sent to the "Palace of Beauties" in a newly constructed area east of the capital. There they were taught singing, dancing, and other techniques to enhance their charms, as well as the rules and protocols of the Wu palace.

Xi Shi and Zheng Dan learned everything quickly. The King of Yue then ordered his minister Fan Li to take them, together with a few other girls and musicians, to present to the King of Wu.

When the contingent got close to the border, Fan Li walked up to Xi Shi. "Xi Shi! Will you pledge allegiance to the King of Yue?"

"All of us have sworn our oath before the King," replied Xi Shi.

"Do you realize that the future of Yue lies in your hands?"

"Yes, I understand.'

"Do you have any ill feelings toward our King? After all, he has sent you on this mission against your will."

"I know the King has no other choice."

"Excellent!" Fan Li said. "With you by his side, the King of Wu will be heading for his downfall!"

Entry into the Wu Palace

Wu Zixu, a native of the state of Chu, was a powerful

minister in the court of the King of Wu, Fu Chai. He had assisted Fu Chai's father, He Lü, to become the King of Wu. At He Lü's death, Wu arranged for Fu Chai to succeed him on the throne. It was mainly due to Wu's efforts that the state of Wu grew strong and prosperous enough to defeat its powerful rivals, Chu and Zhao.

When Fan Li arrived in Wu with the beauties, Wu Zixu hurried to the palace to see Fu Chai. "I am informed that some young maidens and musicians have been presented by the King of Yue. Is that true?"

"Yes," replied Fu Chai. Knowing what Wu Zixu would say next, he hastily added, "I have accepted the gift."

But Wu Zixu had reservations about the gift, and he cited many historical events in which nations had been toppled by a single beautiful woman. King Jie, last ruler of the Xia Dynasty, lost his empire because Mei Xi lured him into a life of utter debauchery. King Zhou, the last ruler of the Shang Dynasty, ended up immolating himself due to his infatuation with Da Ji. King You, the last ruler of the Western Zhou Dynasty, estranged his vassals for the sake of his favorite, Bao Si, and was killed by nomadic invaders.

Fu Chai turned a deaf ear to Wu Zixu's admonition. "Don't worry," he said, "one of these days I will invite you to enjoy the performance of those lovely maidens from Yue!" With this he walked out, leaving Wu Zixu alone in the audience hall. Wu heaved a deep sigh and left with a heavy heart.

After that Fu Chai spent all his days drinking wine and watching song and dance performances by the Yue maidens. By satisfying all his whims, Xi Shi soon established herself in his good graces. Under her influence Fu Chai indulged himself in merrymaking to the neglect of his regal duties. She even tried to stop him from meeting Wu Zixu, and when this proved unsuccessful, she tried to find out what Wu Zixu had told him.

"We are all afraid of Minister Wu!" she once complained to Fu Chai.

"Why?"

"He has a strong distrust of the King of Yue. If you listen to his advice and send us back to Yue, how would I be able to bear the separation? What does King of Yue amount to compared with you? And how can the Yue palace compare with yours in all its splendor? If that day comes, I would rather kill myself in front of you, or jump into a river rather than return to Yue! After I die, my ghost will come back to keep you company!" As she said this, tears welled up in her eyes.

"Don't worry, my love!" Fu Chai comforted her, beating his chest. "As long as I am alive, who can have you sent away? What do I care about Wu Zixu? That old rascal is growing more impertinent with each passing day! He wants a hand in everything, as if the state of Wu belongs to him. Who does he think he is? When he fled his native land to take refuge in Wu, my late father took pity on him and let him stay. Now he considers himself a grand old man who can throw his weight around. Well, someday I'll let him know who is the master!"

Xi Shi looked delighted and relieved. Bowing to Fu Chai to show her gratitude, she said, "That would be great. We have no need to fear anymore!"

With her incomparable beauty and talent, Xi Shi soon had Fu Chai eating out of her hand. He had her by his side from morning till night. She not only fascinated him with her charms, she also impressed him with her unusual aspirations. One day, knitting her brows, she said to him, "I wonder if my lord is acquainted with the situation in the world. Chu has not yet recovered from its defeat. Jin's position as a superpower is already a thing of the past. After the death of its chief minister, Yan Ying, Qi had no talented man worth mentioning. As for Lu, its three most powerful ministers have reduced the duke to a puppet. All over the central plain of China, who can compare with you? If you stay by my side whiling away the time in wine and music instead of going out to fight for fame and glory, people will undoubtedly blame me for weakening your will power. Even if you don't want to glorify your ancestral name, you can at least try to become the overlord of the central plains for my sake. How I long to have a share of your glory!"

These words filled Fu Chai with delight and admiration and he vowed to fight for supremacy over the central plain.

The Death of Zheng Dan

Soon after her arrival in Wu, Zheng Dan fell ill. Xi Shi visited her at every opportunity. Unlike Xi Shi, she failed to arouse Fu Chai's passion. But he did feel a tender affection toward her and did various things to make her happy. Unappeased, Zheng Dan remained listless and unresponsive.

One day Xi Shi came to find Zheng Dan asleep. She sat down quietly. Zheng Dan's cheeks were flushed because of fever, and her breathing was labored. From her half-opened mouth her teeth looked pale and without luster. Gazing at her, Xi Shi began to sob.

Awakened by an attack of severe coughing, Zheng Dan stared at Xi Shi in a daze, then closed her eyes. Her shoulders were caught in spasms, and silent tears rolled down her checks.

"My dear sister!" Xi Shi cried, overcome with sadness. "Don't ruin your health in this way! We must live on till the old despot meets his doom. Then we can go back to our native land, to Zhuluo Village." Her voice was choked with tears.

Just then a palace maid came in to announce that the King of Wu was drinking wine in a newly built tower and wanted Xi Shi for his company.

When Xi Shi rose to go, Zheng Dan took her by both hands. "Dear sister!" she said in a tremulous voice, her eyes fixed on Xi Shi, "Don't forget about me! In this place I have no friend or kin except you. I admire your willpower and your persistence, but our youth ... and everything we have are destroyed by the King of Wu, cast away by the King of Yue...." She broke into sobs and began to spit blood.

Zheng Dan's health quickly deteriorated. A few months later, she died. Fu Chai had her buried on Huangmao Hill and had a temple built in her memory. Sacrifices were offered at the temple regularly.

Lone Fighter in the Wu Palace

Xi Shi was heartbroken over the death of her dear companion. Now she must fulfill her promise to the King of Yue all by herself. First she coaxed Fu Chai out of his melancholy over Zheng Dan's death. Then she encouraged him to flex his military muscle among the neighboring states. With Wu's resources thus depleted, Yue would have a better chance to defeat the King of Wu.

Wen Zhong, who had devised the seven strategies for the King of Yue, then came up with another deadly scheme. In the name of Gou Jian he traveled to the state of Wu to ask for help. Yue had suffered a severe crop failure, he explained, and its people faced starvation. He pleaded for a loan of ten thousand bushels of grain with the promise to return the same amount the following year. Bo Pi, a sycophantic minister, advised Fu Chai to grant the request, but Wu Zixu objected most vigorously. Unable to reach a decision, Fu Chai took up the matter with Xi Shi.

"Why should there be an argument over such a simple matter?" Xi Shi said with a smile. "You must have heard the saying, 'The people are the foundation of the state, and food is the first necessity of the people'. Yue has long pledged allegiance to Wu, therefore the people of Yue should be regarded as your own subjects. Surely you can't bring yourself to let them starve. When Duke Huan of Qi was the overlord in the central plain, he dictated that if one state suffered a crop failure, all the other states must provide relief. Duke Mu of Qin, who presided over the western states, once offered a large amount of grain to famine victims in an enemy state. Don't you want to surpass them in generosity?"

Fu Chai nodded with approval. "Bo Pi and a few others advised me to grant the loan, but none of them could present such a convincing argument. Tomorrow I will inform Wen Zhong of my decision."

Wen Zhong returned with ten thousand bushels of grain to the exultation of Gou Jian and his officials. The grain was distributed among the common people, who thanked their King for saving their lives. The next year Yue enjoyed a bumper harvest. Wen Zhong had ten thousand bushels of the best grain cooked and dried. He then transported them to Wu in person. Fu Chai was much pleased with what he regarded as Yue's good credit, and ordered the returned grain to be used as seeds. Predictably the seeds all decayed in the field, resulting in a great famine. Though upset, Fu Chai suspected no foul play, but blamed the failure on differences in soil and climate between the two states.

Growing impatient, Gou Jian announced his intention to attack Wu. Wen Zhong shook his head. "No, the time is not ripe! For one thing, Wu Zixu is still alive. Moreover, the Wu troops have not recently ventured out to fight in another state." Reluctantly Gou Jian agreed to bide his time and used the interval to further strengthen his own troops.

Afterward Fu Chai launched an attack on the state of Qi, returning in great victory. The expedition was joined by three thousand soldiers from Yue. When Gou Jian arrived in Wu to offer his congratulations, Fu Chai announced at the court, "Everyone here has been duly rewarded for his merits. By sending three thousand men to assist us, the King of Yue also deserves a reward. In the past few years he has proved his loyalty and devotion. I intend to bestow on him a piece of land. What do you say about that?"

"It is a wise decision," the ministers chanted in unison, "to reward a loyal subject!"

Wu Zixu was the only one to raise an objection. "If we don't destroy Yue once and for all," he warned, "they will come to wipe us out one day!"

Sensing Fu Chai's annoyance, Bo Pi put oil on the fire. "If you were truly loyal to Wu," he said to Wu Zixu, "you would not have left your son in Qi!" Touched to the raw, Wu Zixu fell silent. He had entrusted his son to the care of an old friend in the state of Qi while he was there on a mission, because he thought the boy might come to harm in the impending catastrophe. On learning of this, Fu Chai studied the old minister coldly. "For the sake of my late father," he said, "I will not hold you to account. But you must be aware of your misdeed and never come to see me again."

That evening Fu Chai returned to his bedchamber in a bad mood and told Xi Shi about the incident at the court. "That reminds me of a common saying," Xi Shi said. "'If you use a man, trust him; if you distrust a man, don't use him.' If you trust Minister Wu, then you must listen to his counsel. You will have to kill me, a native of Yue, and send an expedition against my homeland." As she said this, she frowned and placed her hand on her bosom with a painful expression.

Fu Chai hastily went up to stroke her bosom. "What are you talking about?" he remonstrated. "Why should I listen to that old fool?"

"If you have no use for him, why do you allow such a treacherous man to live on?" asked Xi Shi. "How can you prevent him from plotting against you?"

Thus prodded, Fu Chai sent an envoy to Wu Zixu with a sword. Wu Zixu took the sword in hand and turned to his servants. "After I die," he said, "pluck out my eyes and hang them at the city gate, so that I can watch the Yue troops marching in!" Then he cut his throat. Informed of Wu Zixu's last words, Fu Chai ordered his body thrown into the river. "What can you see now, old fool?" he taunted.

After Wu Zixu's death no one was left in the court to advise Fu Chai against his excesses. To please Xi Shi he had a new palace built for her and spent night and day with her in endless orgies and dissipation. When he began construction of a terrace on Gusu Hill, Gou Jian immediately sent some huge logs to Wu as a present. Though pleased with the unusual size of the logs, Fu Chai was not sure he should change the construction plan to make use of them. "One should not put fine timber to petty use," Xi Shi advised him. "The Gusu terrace should be very high and very wide. Otherwise how can it symbolize the greatness of our nation?" Fu Chai nodded his assent.

Numerous laborers were conscripted to undertake the gargantuan construction project. Weighed down by the heavy burden, the people of Wu seethed in discontent.

A Fable Told to Deaf Ears

After Wu Zixu's death, Fu Chai appointed Bo Pi as his chief minister. To compete for regional hegemony, he again conscripted a large number of laborers to dig a canal connecting the Yangtze River with the Huaihe River. Sailing upstream with his troops, he inflicted a crushing defeat on the state of Qi at Ailing. Back from this victory, he conscripted yet more laborers to further extend the canal. With the project completed, the state of Wu would have a water route leading directly to the central plains of China. However, the resources of the state were exhausted in the process of digging the canal.

Many court officials became aware of the coming crisis, but none dared speak for fear of sharing Wu Zixu's fate. Fu Chai's son, Prince You, finally came up with an idea. One day he came to see his father with a slingshot in his hand, his clothes wet and soiled.

"I was playing in the garden this morning," he explained to the astonished king, "when I saw a cicada crouching on the highest branch of a tree. It was singing happily, as if there weren't a care in the world. Little did it expect that a giant mantis, raising its claws, was approaching stealthily from behind. The mantis looked upon the cicada as a fine meal, but it was unaware of an oriole about to swoop down on it. I brought out my slingshot and took my aim, but I was too intent on the oriole to notice a pit overgrown with weeds, so I tripped and fell into it before I could shoot the bird."

Fu Chai burst out laughing. "No one can be more foolish than you!" he said. "To fall into a pit trying to shoot a bird!"

Prince You abruptly fell on his knees. "It was indeed foolish of me to ignore the pit trying to shoot the bird, to forget peril in the prospect of gain, and for this folly I suffered the consequences. But there is someone even more foolish than I!"

"Who can that be?"

"I don't dare to mention his name without your promise to spare my life."

"I promise you. You won't be blamed whatever name you mention."

"It is you, father!" The prince burst into tears and lowered his head.

"What?" Fu Chai's eyes bulged in anger. "How could it be me? Tell me why, you rascal! If you can't come up with a good reason, I'll have you be beheaded!"

"The cicada was singing to its heart's content, with no intention of fighting with anyone. Little did it expect an attack from its enemy, the mantis. The mantis, on the other hand, was too eager to eat the cicada to notice the oriole. As for the oriole, it was totally unaware that I was about to shoot it. And I was unaware of the existence of the pit, so I fell into it. The cicada, the mantis, and the oriole were greedy and foolish, and so was I. But the object of my greed was nothing more than a bird, and I only fell into the pit because of my foolishness. But who would expect a sovereign to make the same mistake as the cicada, the mantis, and the oriole?

The Duke of Lu, for instance, did nothing to better the livelihood of his people or enhance the power of his troops. Therefore he was unable to repel the invading army of Qi and had to ask us for help. The Duke of Qi, on the other hand, was so eager to savor the sweet sensation of conquest that he overlooked the threat posed by Wu. As for you, father, you have an ambitious plan of bringing the entire central plain under submission, and for this purpose you are ready to launch an expedition against Qi by stretching our financial and military capacity to its limit. However, you seem to have forgotten about Yue. To avenge his ignominious defeat many years ago the King of Yue won't hesitate to seize this opportunity to attack us. His army would sweep across our territory, massacre our people, burn our ancestral temples and palace buildings to the ground, and seize control of our land!

"Surely the sovereigns of Lu and Qi are foolish, but their folly pales in comparison with yours. By launching the expedition you would make yourself the most foolish man under heaven! The state of Wu has been pushed to the edge of a bottomless pit, which is a thousand times more perilous than the one into which I fell today. With our nation destroyed, no more sacrifices would be offered at the shrine of our ancestors, and our people would be plunged into complete misery. Please think about this!"

The prince prostrated himself on the ground and broke into loud wails. Touched by his sincerity, Fu Chai said, "All right, I won't punish you today. I will give your words some consideration. You may leave now."

Despite his son's exhortations, Fu Chai finally decided to march north to attack Qi, a move applauded by Xi Shi. The expedition itself was highly successful. However, with the best troops gone, defense at the Wu capital was weak. At last Gou Jian saw the chance he had been waiting for all these years. The Yue army launched a surprise attack, fighting all the way to the Wu capital. Fu Chai returned in haste to relieve the siege, but his tired and demoralized troops could not beat off the men of Yue. Thus he was compelled to sue for peace. From then on Yue grew steadily in strength and inflicted several defeats on Wu.

One day Xi Shi knelt before Fu Chai, sword in hand, begging to be punished with death. Fu Chai helped her to her feet and comforted her kindly. "You have done nothing wrong. Why should I want to kill you?"

"The King of Yue has betrayed you. As a native of Yue I am guilty of treason."

"Nonsense!" Fu Chai cried. "No one can choose where to be born. I don't regard every native of Yue as my enemy. Since you are not Gou Jian's daughter, why should you be responsible for his offense? Come on, don't talk about this anymore. Let's empty our cups together!" After that Fu Chai was too dispirited to attend to state affairs. Most of his time was spent in drinking wine with Xi Shi.

Gou Jian had no intention of giving Wu any breathing space. Together with Fan Li and Wen Zhong, he led the Yue troops on an all-out offensive against Wu. After losing several battles, Fu Chai retreated to the capital and sent an envoy to sue for peace. This time Gou Jian refused adamantly. The envoy shuttled between the two armies, paying Gou Jian a total of seven visits, but to no avail. For some time the Wu capital withstood the siege. Then Bo Pi surrendered, opening the city gate to the Yue troops. Escorted by a few followers, Fu Chai fled into the Zhiyang Mountain, with the Yue troops close at his heels. Fu Chai realized there was no escape. "I cannot face Wu Zixu in the underworld!" he told his followers with a sigh. "Please cover my face with a piece of cloth." Then he drew his sword and cut his own throat.

For Gou Jian, the euphoria over the conquest of Wu had no effect on his distrustful character. He began to regard Fan Li and Wen Zhong with dark suspicion, fearing that capable men like them might challenge his authority. Aware of his precarious position, Fan Li decided to flee. He tried to talk Wen Zhong into going with him, saying, "The King of Yue is a man with whom you can share misfortunes but not success." Wen Zhong, however, was unconvinced.

Fan Li therefore left Gou Jian without saying good-bye, but Wen Zhong did not follow suit. One day Gou Jian said to him, "You taught me seven strategies, and I destroyed Wu by employing four of them. Why don't you go and recommend the other three to my late father?" He then gave Wen Zhong the sword with which Wu Zixu had committed suicide, and Wen Zhong came to the same end.

With Fan Li and Wen Zhong out of the way, Gou Jian began to think of Xi Shi, who had gone into hiding when the Wu capital was first put under siege. Gou Jian's men found her and brought her before him. "You have done a lot for our nation," Gou Jian told her. "What do you want as a reward?"

"Nothing," replied Xi Shi. "I stayed in the Wu palace for ten years only avenge the insult of my lord's imprisonment in Wu and the sufferings of my countrymen inflicted by the Wu invaders. Now that I have completed my mission, I won't ask for any reward, but I would be content if allowed to return to Zhuluo Village where I can live a simple life washing cloth and spinning silk."

Gou Jian was impressed. After so many years, Xi Shi still retained her ravishing beauty. Gou Jian had given her up in order to defeat Wu. Now, at last, he could take her as his own concubine.

Gou Jian's wife, the Queen, burned with jealousy on learning that he was returning to Yue with Xi Shi. She sent some men to spread rumors describing Xi Shi as a vicious woman who would ruin the King of Yue just as she had ruined Fu Chai. Then she had Xi Shi tied into a leather bag and drowned in a river. The renowned beauty who had toppled a nation thus came to a miserable end.

43

DESPOTIC EMPRESS LÜ

Lü Zhi married Liu Bang when he was a petty official. Liu Bang later founded the Han empire and ruled it from 206 to 193 B.C. For many years she had to do household chores and even toil in the fields. She gave birth to a son and a daughter. At that time the Emperor of Qin was losing control of his empire as rebellions broke out from all sides. Liu Bang joined the rank of the rebels and steadily built up his own forces. The collapse of the Qin Dynasty was followed by a fierce contention for supremacy among the anti-Qin military leaders. By employing talented men and gaining widespread support among the people through his benign policies, Liu Bang emerged as the final victor. He was later known as Emperor Gaozu. Lü Zhi became the empress, and her son, Liu Ying, the crown prince.

Consolidating the Heir Apparent's Position

Liu Ying's position as the crown prince was far from secure. Liu Bang's favorite concubine, Lady Qi, bore him a son named Ruyi, who was enfeoffed as the Prince of Zhao. Liu Bang thought that Ruyi really took after him, so Ruyi became his favorite son. On the other hand, he disliked Liu Ying, who was kind and timid in character. Aware of the emperor's partiality, Lady Qi urged him to replace Liu Ying with Ruyi as his successor.

One day in the autumn of 197 B.C. Liu Bang summoned an audience in the main hall of Weiyang Palace. He told the civil and military officials that he had reached an important decision and would like to listen to their opinions about it. Lü Zhi, who had a vague sense of some impending catastrophe, eavesdropped at the eastern chamber adjacent to the hall when Liu Bang addressed his ministers.

Liu Bang twitched his nose and stroked his long beard, and then said, "The crown prince is too weak and incompetent to succeed to the throne." He glanced at the ministers, who were listening with rapt attention. "Ruyi, the Prince of Zhao, is intelligent and capable despite his tender age. Moreover, he takes after me in the way he speaks and conducts himself. Therefore I intend to deprive Liu Ying of the title of crown prince and give it to Ruyi. What do you think?"

At these words Lü Zhi was convulsed with anger and jealousy. She became so dizzy in the head and weak in the limbs that she nearly fainted. Closing her eyes, she leaned against the wall and forced herself to calm down so that she could listen to the ministers' comments.

Liu Bang's pronouncement took the ministers by surprise. Most of them spoke against deposing the crown prince, but Liu Bang turned a deaf ear to their objections. Just then Zhou Chang stepped forth to speak. He was a long-time follower of Liu Bang and was well acquainted with the root of the problem. He knew that Lady Qi, a beautiful young woman with a sweet voice and superb dancing skills, had been picked up by Liu Bang when he was retreating after a lost battle. Infatuated with her, Liu Bang kept Lady Qi by his side all the years he was fighting his way to the throne. In the meantime Lü Zhi had stayed behind and thus grew estranged from her husband.

When Liu Bang saw Zhou Chang kneeling before him, he was a bit uneasy, for this was not an easy man to deal with. On one occasion, Zhou Chang had burst into the rear palace to make an urgent report, only to find the emperor drunk with Lady Qi in his arms. He was about to slip away when Liu Bang caught sight of him and told him to stay. Pushing Lady Qi aside, Liu Bang got up and walked briskly toward Zhou Chang, who hastily knelt in salute. With liquor welling up in his head, Liu Bang on impulse sat astride on Zhou Chang's neck and tauntingly asked him, "Tell me, what sort of emperor am I?" Not a bit intimidated and straining to raise his head, Zhou Chang muttered, "Your Majesty is ... is just like the despotic King Jie of Xia and King Zhou of Shang, both of whom came to a miserable end!" This sent Liu Bang into a fit of laughter. Leaping to his feet, he told Zhou Chang to stand up, listened to his report, and sent him away. After that incident Liu Bang was always somewhat on guard in Zhou Chang's presence.

With Zhou Chang now kneeling before him, Liu Bang was compelled to ask his opinion.

Zhou Chang was so agitated that his lips trembled without producing a sound. Finally he stuttered, "Though I c-cannot speak well, I know it's o-out of the question! If Your Majesty wants to depose the crown prince, I will refuse to obey!" Liu Bang roared with laughter at Zhou Chang's stuttering, indignant voice. The other ministers also laughed, which relieved the tension at the court, and Liu Bang decided to put the matter aside for the time being in the face of such strong opposition.

The audience over, the ministers streamed out of the hall with Zhou Chang at the end of the train. Lü Zhi suddenly emerged from the eastern chamber and accosted him. Before Zhou Chang could salute her, she fell on her knees, saying, in thanks, "Without you, the crown prince would have been deposed today!"

"I didn't do it for your sake," said Zhou Chang, "but for the sake of our country!" With a sweep of his sleeves, he walked away.

Gazing after him, Lü Zhi was in a daze for a moment, and then she broke into a cold smile. A weight had been lifted from her chest. As long as the crown prince retained his position, supreme power of the imperial court would fall into her hands sooner or later.

In the winter of 196 B.C. Liu Bang led an expedition to suppress a revolt and returned with an arrow wound in his chest. As the injury worsened, he feared that his days were numbered and again talked about deposing the crown prince. But again he met with strong opposition from his ministers, including his ablest advisor, Zhang Liang. Unable to dissuade him, Zhang Liang stopped attending audiences, pleading illness. A minister named Shusun Tong gave Liu Bang a lengthy discourse on the perils of replacing the crown prince, citing many historical examples, and threatening to commit suicide if the emperor should execute his plan. Highly displeased, Liu Bang again put the matter on the shelf.

Apprehensive for her son's future, Lü Zhi now went to Zhang Liang to seek his advice. "To dissuade His Majesty, something other than verbal arguments are needed," Zhang Liang said. "In the Shangshan Mountain there are four old hermits widely respected for their virtue and talents. They have declined the emperor's invitation to serve in the court because they find him arrogant and uncivil. However, the crown prince, with a hand-written letter and munificent gifts, may be able to convince the four old men to leave the mountain and keep him company. When he enters the court on a formal occasion, he can bring them along with him, Then when His Majesty finds out that the crown prince has the four hermits from Shangshan Mountain in his service, he will be forced to abandon the plan." Lü Zhi accepted Zhang Liang's advice with delight.

One day Liu Bang gave a feast for his family in the front hall of Weiyang Palace. Smiling broadly, he accepted toasts from the various princes. Then he noticed the four gray-haired men, who seemed to be in their eighties, in the company of the crown prince. "Who are you?" he demanded, pointing at them with his finger.

When the four old men calmly gave their names, Liu Bang's eyes widened in astonishment. "I sent men to fetch you several times, but you always evaded me. Why have you come with the crown prince today?"

"Because Your Majesty has rude manners," they replied, "we would fain live as hermits in the mountain than serve as officials in the court. But the crown prince has a reputation for benevolence and modesty. People all across the empire are eager to be of service to him. Therefore we have come to assist him."

Liu Bang sighed deeply. "Take good care of the crown prince," he told them. Dispirited by this incident, he left at once for his bedchamber.

At the sight of the glum look on Liu Bang's face, Lady Qi immediately went to wait on him with tender solicitude. Liu Bang felt a surge of sadness as he gazed at her lovely face and alluring figure. "I want to make your son my heir, but the crown prince has consolidated his position by enlisting the four grand old men from Shangshan Mountain into his service. The situation is beyond remedy. I'm afraid Lü Zhi has gained the upper hand." At his words Lady Qi began to shed tears of despair. "Stop crying," said Liu Bang, trying to console her. "I will try my best to secure your future. Come on, dance a Chu-style dance for me, and I'll sing a Chu song!" Lady Qi brushed away her tears with a silk handkerchief and performed a slow dance, moving her feet and swaying her waist, while Liu Bang beat the rhythm with his fingers and sang in accompaniment.

After the dance Lady Qi resumed her crying. Gazing at her, Liu Bang heaved long sighs but could find nothing to say. In the meantime Lü Zhi was rejoicing over her triumph. After that, Liu Bang made no more attempts to replace her son with the son of his favorite consort.

Supreme General Han Xin Is Decapitated

In the autumn of 197 B.C. a contingent of footmen and cavalry poured out of Luoyang, the imperial capital of Han. Dressed in a suit of armor, Liu Bang sat on a horse with a tired look on his face. His empress and court officials went out of the city to see him off. "I entrust the affairs of the court to you," he said to Lü Zhi. "If you are uncertain about anything, consult Chief Minister Xiao." At this Xiao He, who was standing near the empress, bowed respectfully.

Liu Bang was leading an expedition against Chen Xi, who had raised a revolt at Daidi. Chen Xi, who had been one of Liu Bang's meritorious generals, had been appointed to the garrison at Daidi. Before his departure he paid a visit to Han Xin, the Marquis of Huaiyin. They were good friends and shared their grievances against Liu Bang for his intense mistrust of the generals who had assisted him in unifying the empire. Then, on his arrival at Daidi, Chen Xi began to make friends with the local strongmen and to enlist the services of talented people. Several Han generals who had defected to the Huns contacted him in secret, and a few wealthy merchants offered their allegiance. Thereupon Chen Xi proclaimed himself Prince of Dai, attacking and capturing many cities. Flying into a rage, Liu Bang decided to vanquish the rebels in person.

Clasping his hands in front of his chest as a farewell gesture, Liu Bang rode off, escorted by the imperial guards. It took a long time for the dust to settle after the army left. Lü Zhi gazed after the expedition until it nearly vanished out of sight, then mounted her chariot to return to the palace. Her mind was busily working on a scheme to get rid of Supreme General Han Xin, who was a thorn in her side and, she suspected, a danger to Liu Bang.

Han Xin had played a decisive role in the contention between Liu Bang and his powerful rival, Xiang Yu. Xiao He recognized his military genius and recommended him to Liu Bang, who appointed him supreme general. Gaining one victory after another, Han Xin shifted the balance of power in favor of Liu Bang, and the territory under Han control expanded steadily. Finally, in a great battle at Gaixia, Han Xin inflicted a crushing defeat on Xiang Yu's troops. In despair, Xiang Yu cut his own throat. This put an end to the four-year civil war, and China became once again unified under the Han Dynasty.

When the civil war was reaching a crucial point, Xiang Yu sent envoys to Han Xin to try to make him change his allegiance. Han Xin had such strong forces under his command that he was in a position to decide the outcome of the war. He was reminded by Xiang Yu's envoys that if he should succeed in defeating Xiang Yu, he would then become useless to Liu Bang and would be eliminated in his turn. But Han Xin turned down Xiang Yu's offer, saying he could not bring himself to betray Liu Bang, who had made him supreme general when he was a person in total obscurity. Some of Han Xin's followers also advised him to leave Liu Bang and declare independence, thus carving up the country with Liu Bang and Xiang Yu, but he would not listen to them either.

After his ascension to the throne, Liu Bang began to treat Han Xin with mounting suspicion and animosity. Han Xin was deprived of his general's seal and relieved of his military command. On one occasion he was suddenly arrested on a charge of treason. Later he was released because of lack of evidence, but he was then demoted from the rank of prince to that of marquis.

Nevertheless, Lü Zhi continued to regard Han Xin as a serious menace and wanted to eliminate him. When someone reported to her that Han Xin had visited Chen Xi to plot revolt, she immediately sent for Chief Minister Xiao He. Together they worked out a plan to trap Han Xin.

One day a horseman, one of Lü Zhi's henchmen, galloped into the capital, claiming to have come from the northern frontier with the emperor's message about a great victory. According to the horseman, Chen Xi had been killed, and the emperor was heading back to the capital.

The court officials, all kept in the dark, went to the palace one after another to offer their congratulations. But Han Xin was suspicious, so he did not show up. Lü Zhi had to send

Xiao He to invite him.

"His Majesty has gained a resounding victory," Xiao He told Han Xin. "All the ministers have been to the palace to offer congratulations except you. You are courting public criticism by your careless conduct. How will you explain it to His Majesty on his return?" Reluctantly Han Xin came with Xiao He to the palace. Stepping inside the gate, he was seized by palace guards, tied up and brought to Lü Zhi.

Lü Zhi glared at him. "Why did you plot a revolt with Chen Xi?"

Han Xin did not kneel in salute. His head cocked up, he replied calmly, "This is a rumor."

Lü Zhi sneered. "Someone has betrayed you! Don't try to deny your guilt!" Turning to the guards, she ordered, "Take him out and behead him!"

Han Xin realized there was no use in pleading his innocence. Looking upward, he heaved a deep sigh. "When high-flying birds are out, the strong bow will be tucked away; when fast-running rabbits are out, the hunting dog will be cooked; when enemy states are conquered, the generals will be beheaded. I have served His Majesty with unswerving devotion for many years. Now I regret not having listened to better advice. After my death, your days will be numbered!"

Lü Zhi flushed with fury. "Take him away!" she bellowed. "Off with his head!"

After Han Xin was killed, Lü Zhi had all members from the families of his father, mother, and wife arrested and executed. When Liu Bang finally returned with victory, he was immensely relieved on learning Han Xin's death, though at the same time he felt a sense of loss. After all, Han Xin had been his most capable general.

The Non-Liu Princes Are Eliminated

Along the thoroughfare leading from the imperial capital to Sichuan, a carriage moved at a slow pace. Sitting in it was

Peng Yue, the former Prince of Liang. He had just been deprived of his noble title and exiled to the remote area of Sichuan. Naturally he looked haggard and gloomy.

Peng Yue was one of Liu Bang's chief generals. During the civil war he had led his troops in diversionary actions behind enemy lines. He had also joined the decisive battle at Gaixia, contributing to Liu Bang's final victory. After Liu Bang became emperor, Peng Yue was invested as the Prince of Liang because of his merits. However, he pleaded illness when Liu Bang summoned him for the expedition against Chen Xi. His suspicion aroused, Liu Bang reduced Peng to the status of a commoner.

When Peng Yue arrived at Zhengxian County, he happened to meet Lü Zhi on her way back from Chang'an. Looking deeply concerned, she asked, "Where are you heading, General Peng?"

Touched by her solicitude, Peng Yue poured out his grievances to her. "For all these years I fought by His Majesty's side to unify the empire and achieved merits with my sweat and blood. Please ask His Majesty to spare me the banishment and let me spend my remaining years in my hometown. I would be grateful to you forever!"

"How I sympathize with you, General Peng! I will do my best to help you. Don't go to Sichuan. Return to the capital with me, and I will speak to the emperor in your favor."

Overjoyed, Peng Yue followed Lü Zhi back to Luoyang.

On her return to the palace, Lü Zhi went straight to see Liu Bang. "Peng Yue is a great warrior," she said. "Why did you exile him to Sichuan? I have brought him back."

"Why?" Liu Bang asked in surprise.

Lü Zhi's lips twitched to suppress a smile. "If you want to punish him, make sure you do it thoroughly. You deprived him of his rank and post but spared him his life. He might be able to build up his strength and raise a revolt." Lü Zhi stepped up to Liu Bang and lowered her voice. "Let's have him executed on a charge of treason. In that way we can rid ourselves of a potential threat and frighten the other ministers into awe and submission."

Liu Bang stopped stroking his beard. After a long pause, he nodded his assent.

By Lü Zhi's arrangement, someone stood forth to accuse Peng Yue of plotting a revolt. Peng Yue was found guilty and executed along with families of his father, mother and wife. To scare the other princes into total submission, Lü Zhi had Peng Yue's body chopped into pieces, cooked into a stew and distributed among the princes.

On receiving his share of the stew, Ying Bu, the Prince of Huainan, trembled in horror. With Han Xin and Peng Yue dead, he would undoubtedly become the next victim. He decided, therefore, to take preemptive action by staging a rebellion.

When news of this rebellion reached the capital, Liu Bang at first intended to send the crown prince on an pacifying expedition, but Lü Zhi advised against it. "We should not underestimate Ying Bu, who is a battle-seasoned general. Besides, the generals in the expedition have all fought by your side; how can you expect them to submit willingly to the command of the crown prince? That would be putting a sheep in command of a pack of wolves. On the other hand, by leading the expedition in person, you can make the generals do their best even if you just lie in the carriage all day."

Liu Bang frowned with displeasure. "All right," he said finally. "Since the crown prince is incompetent, I suppose I have to fight the rebels myself."

After several major battles Liu Bang defeated Ying Bu. However, Liu Bang received an arrow wound in the chest that took a long time to heal. On his return he summoned all the ministers to a meeting. A white horse was slain, with everyone smearing its blood on their mouths in token of an oath: "No one outside the Liu family can be a prince, and no one without achieving merits can receive a noble title. If anyone should break this oath, all people under heaven shall rise up against him." In this way Liu Bang managed to put his own family in firm control of the empire. Little did he suspect that Lü Zhi, his empress, was building up her own power base in preparation for a takeover.

The Tragic End of Lady Qi

In the fourth month of 195 B.C. Liu Bang died of illness in the palace. With her followers, Lü Zhi worked out a plan to seize supreme power for herself. According to the plan, they would keep the emperor's death a secret, summon the ministers and generals into the palace one by one, and kill them all. However, her nephew, whom she had taken into her confidence, revealed the plot after getting tipsy at his dinner table. Lü Zhi was compelled to announce the emperor's death. Liu Ying, the crown prince, ascended the throne, with Lü Zhi elevated to the status of empress dowager.

Liu Ying, or Emperor Huidi, was such a weakling that he submitted the imperial power to Lü Zhi without a fight. At last she could vent her pent-up rage on Lady Qi and her son, Ruyi. Lady Qi was locked up. Dressed in a prison uniform, she was made to grind rice as a slave all day. As the late emperor's favorite consort, Lady Qi found the hardship and humiliation too hard to bear. While grinding the rice, she began to sing in a tearful voice:

> The son a prince,
> The mother a slave,
> To grind rice from dawn till dusk,
> With death waiting at the door.
> You are three thousand li away;
> How can I pass my message to you?

Informed of the song, Lü Zhi muttered furiously, "So you still fancy your son will come to your rescue?" She immediately sent an envoy to fetch Ruyi, the Prince of Zhao. Some years before, Liu Bang had appointed Zhou Chang to be Ruyi's grand councillor. Zhou Chang was aware of Lü Zhi's ill intentions, and he would not let Ruyi leave his fiefdom, so the prince declined Lü Zhi's summons three times. When she found out about this, Lü Zhi ordered Zhou Chang to come to the capital first, then sent for the prince again, saying that his mother missed him badly. Without Zhou Chang by his side, the teenaged prince set out for the capital at once.

Ruyi was welcomed to the capital by Emperor Huidi himself, who escorted him into the palace. The kind-hearted emperor did not approve of his mother's ill treatment of Lady Qi. For fear that Ruyi might come to harm, the emperor bade him stay in his own bedchamber and shared every meal with him. As a result, Lü Zhi did not have a chance to harm the prince.

Then, on a cold winter morning, Ruyi, who was a teenager fond of long sleep, failed to get up early. Emperor Huidi did not try to wake him up but went out to practice archery by himself. In the interval, the prince was poisoned to death by an envoy from Lü Zhi. On his return, Emperor Huidi burst into tears over Ruyi's body. Though he knew from where the assassin had come, he did not dare hold his mother to account. Ruyi was buried in the manner befitting a prince.

Having gotten Ruyi out of the way, Lü Zhi no longer wanted to have his mother grinding rice. What she had in mind for her long-time enemy was the cruelest torture imaginable. Lady Qi's limbs were cut off, with the remaining parts the same length as a pig's feet. Her eyes were gouged out, her ears smoked deaf, and her mouth drugged dumb. Lü Zhi then had her fenced into a corner like a pig and named her "the pig-woman."

When Lü Zhi displayed her victim to Emperor Huidi, he screamed in horror. He felt so weak in the knees that he nearly fell to the ground. Supported by palace attendants, he returned to his chamber and became bed-ridden. He had someone pass on this message to his mother: "This is not what a human should be capable of doing. As the empress dowager's son, I am no longer entitled to rule the empire." After recovering from his illness, the emperor lost all interest in state affairs. It seemed that he no longer cared about anything, but wanted to escape from the cruel world. He began to lead a dissipated life, indulging in wine and women and neglecting his regal duties. Lü Zhi took over control of the imperial court with great satisfaction.

Presiding over the Court

After several years of utter debauchery, Emperor Huidi died prematurely at the age of twenty-four. Lü Zhi did not show any sign of grief, much to the puzzlement of the court ministers. A palace attendant named Zhang Piqiang asked Chief Minister Chen Ping, "The empress dowager must be overcome with sorrow over the loss of her only son, but she has not shed a single drop of tears. Do you know the reason behind this?"

"Frankly, I don't," replied Chen Ping.

"At the emperor's demise, the heir apparent is too young to succeed to the throne. The empress dowager is therefore regarding the ministers with deep suspicion. That's why she does not weep in spite of her grief. Do you think she will spare those she strongly distrusts?"

Chen Ping grew anxious. "What can we do to protect ourselves?" he asked.

Zhang Piqiang had apparently already worked it out. "It would be advisable for you to advise the empress dowager to appoint her two nephews generals and put them in command of the palace guards as well as the troops in the capital. Then you can recommend people from the Lü family to be high officials. In that way the empress dowager will be appeased and feel secure, and the ministers will not come to harm."

Failing to come up with a better idea, Chen Ping acted on Zhang's advice. Lü Zhi granted his request at once, putting her own nephews in charge of the armed forces in the capital. Only then did she give vent to her grief, weeping and wailing for her lost son.

The heir apparent, Liu Gong, was enthroned. As he was still a baby, Lü Zhi became the de facto ruler of the Han empire. To consolidate her position, she intended to invest some of her family members as princes. When she took up the subject at an audience, Chief Minister Wang Ling, a quick-tongued man, spoke up in objection. "No one outside the Liu family can be made a prince!" he blurted out. "All of us swore such an oath with Emperor Gaozu!"

Feeling affronted, Lü Zhi turned to ask Chen Ping and Zhou Bo. "What do you think?"

"When Emperor Gaozu unified the empire, he had the right to invest his family members as princes if he liked. Now that you are presiding over the court, there is nothing wrong in making your own family members princes."

After the audience, Wang Ling remonstrated with Chen Ping and Zhou Bo. "Didn't you swear the oath with Emperor Gaozu?" he demanded. "Instead of preventing the empress dowager from breaking the oath, you uttered sweet nonsense to curry favor with her. Won't you be too ashamed to meet Emperor Gaozu in the underworld?"

Unperturbed, Chen Ping and Zhou Bo replied, "We admire your courage to speak your mind at court. But as to safeguarding the rights of the imperial family, you won't contribute as much as we will."

Soon after, Wang Ling was demoted to be the emperor's tutor.

Lü Zhi ruled the empire for eight years. She conferred royal titles first on her deceased father and elder brother, then on her nephews and their children. Lü Can and Lü Lu also became generals in charge of the imperial guards in the palace.

Lü Zhi held a stable position and began to act more and more unscrupulously.

The Ploughing Rhyme

Lü Zhi tried to bring all the princes with the family name of Liu under her submission by marrying daughters from the Lü family to them. Both Liu You, Prince of Zhao, and Liu Hui, Prince of Liang, had women named Lü for their principal wives.

Estranged from his wife, Liu You spent all his days in the company of his favorite concubines. Burning with jealousy, his wife brought a trumped-up charge against him. According to her, Liu You had once remarked, "How can the Lüs become princes! When the empress dowager is dead, I will wipe them out." Thus he was thrown into prison and given nothing to eat. Consumed by hunger, he began to sing a self-composed song to vent his indignation. Finally he starved to death.

Liu Hui, the Prince of Liang, married the daughter of Lü Zhi's nephew, Lü Can. She became the head of the family, dictating whatever he should or should not do. When he showed the slightest partiality toward a concubine, she would immediately have the woman poisoned to death. At the end of six months Liu Hui committed suicide in despair.

Liu Zhang, invested as the Marquis of Zhuxu, was a hefty warrior. He married the daughter of Lü Zhi's nephew, Lü Lu. Dissatisfied with the excesses of the Lü family, he tried to find an opportunity to get even with them.

One evening the palace was alight with lanterns and candlelight. Lü Zhi was giving a banquet to her family, some Liu princes, and a few ministers including Chen Ping and Zhou Bo. Everyone had a small table laid out with wine and dishes.

Seated in the place of honor, Lü Zhi had a big smile on her face. She looked around at her guests and announced, "I feel so happy today, so I am giving this family banquet. You don't have to stand on ceremony."

"A banquet can never do without a supervising officer," remarked one of her nephews.

"All right," Lü Zhi said, and her eyes fell on Liu Zhang, who was tall, handsome and well-mannered. "Let's have the Marquis of Zhuxu for our supervising officer!"

Liu Zhang rose from his seat and went up to Lü Zhi, holding a wine pot in one hand and the handle of his sword in the other. "I come from a general's family," he said, "so please let me supervise the banquet by martial law."

In her unusually jovial mood Lü Zhi did not suspect anything. "Granted," she said. "A supervising officer must be strict. If anyone tries to leave early, you don't need ask my permission to behead them!"

After a few rounds of wine, Liu Zhang went up to Lü Zhi. "Your humble subject offers to sing a ploughing rhyme to add to the fun."

Lü Zhi nodded her assent. Liu Zhang then cleared his throat and began to sing while clapping his hands:

Plough deep, water the seeds,
And weed the field when crop sprouts.
Root out all those plants
Intruding on your field!

Lü Zhi changed her countenance and threw a glance at her family members. Some were wolfing down their meals, some were drinking wine, and one of them were applauding Liu Zhang, shouting "Excellent! Let's have one more!"

"A bunch of idiots!" she swore to herself. "Liu Zhang implied in his song that my family have taken control of the empire and should be wiped out like weeds. None of them got the message!" She then left the banquet hall so as not to show her displeasure, knowing the undertone of a song could not be used to incriminate Liu Zhang.

The feast went on uninterrupted. After a while one of the

Lüs, getting tipsy, slipped out of the hall. Liu Zhang seized this long-awaited opportunity by racing out and in a moment returning with a bloody head in his left hand and a blood-stained sword in the right. "A man left the feast without permission," he reported to Lü Zhi. "I have beheaded him according to martial law."

The Lüs were stupefied and trembled with fear, and Lü Zhi realized she had been trapped. As Liu Zhang had received her mandate, she was unable to find fault with him. She was well aware that Liu Zhang was not the only person hostile toward the Lü family. She had to be constantly on guard against such ill will from all sides.

Weighed down by anxiety and overstrain, Lü Zhi fell terminally ill the following year (180 B.C.). On her deathbed she appointed Lü Can chief minister and Lü Lu supreme general, and set up Lü Lu's daughter as the empress. "When I die," she warned them, "the ministers may stage a coup at my funeral. Do not take part in the funeral procession, but stay in the palace and put the guards on alert. Give the assassins no chance to get close to you." These were her last words.

At Lü Zhi's death, Chen Ping and Zhou Bo seized control of the imperial army and joined forces with Liu Xiang and Liu Zhang to wipe out the Lü family. Liu Heng, one of Liu Bang's sons, was put on the throne. Known as Emperor Wendi, he ushered in a period of peace and prosperity for the Han Dynasty.

WANG ZHI BECOMES EMPRESS BY HER SECOND MARRIAGE

In ancient China there was a woman who became empress by her second marriage. After marrying a commoner and bearing him a daughter, she was selected to enter the imperial palace where she rose to the top of her peers. Her son, Liu Che, was Emperor Wudi, renowned in history for his military exploits.

Lady Wang Bears the Emperor a Son

In the Qiyi Hall of the Han palace, Lady Wang stood gazing at the goldfish in the pond, her mind churning. Liu Qi, or Emperor Jingdi, had just deposed his empress, Lady Bo. Who would be chosen to replace her? Lady Li seemed to be the most likely candidate. She was the favorite of Emperor Jingdi, who had designated her son, Liu Rong, as the heir apparent. When he deposed Lady Bo, the emperor must have had Lady Li in mind.

"How can I become empress myself?" Lady Wang wondered.

Lady Wang, whose given name was Zhi, had a daughter by her first marriage with a commoner. When the court ordered a selection of beautiful maidens for the imperial princes, she deserted her husband and child and left for the palace, where she was assigned to Liu Qi, the heir apparent. By virtue of her good looks and womanly charms, she became the prince's favorite. Soon after, her younger sister also entered palace, at her recommendation, to wait upon Liu Qi.

After his ascension, Liu Qi dreamed one night of a red pig descending from heaven and heading for the Qiyi Hall. Waking early in the morning, he hastened to the Hall and found it shrouded in purple clouds shaped like a dragon. To find out the message of the dream he consulted an augur, who pronounced it an auspicious dream signifying that a prince would be born in the hall who would become heir to the throne. Some days later Liu Qi had another dream in which a goddess handed Lady Wang a sun, which she promptly swallowed. When he described the dream to her, Lady Wang said she had dreamed the same dream. Thereupon Liu Qi had her moved into the Qiyi Hall. Soon afterwards she gave birth to a son, who was named Liu Che.

Having borne an imperial prince, Lady Wang was more than ever resolved to compete for the title of empress with Lady Li. She did not take any rash actions but waited patiently for the opportunity to arise.

Lady Li Misses Her Chance

For Lady Li, the position of empress seemed to be within easy reach.

The former empress, Lady Bo, had married Liu Qi when he was the crown prince and had received the title princess-consort. Though he never particularly liked her, Liu Qi was compelled to make her empress when he succeeded to the throne. Her position, however, was precarious not only because she was out of favor with the emperor, but also because she had no child. After Lady Li's son was made heir apparent, Lady Li strained every nerve to weaken the empress' position. Finally Lady Bo was deposed and sent to live in a secluded corner of the palace.

With the empress deposed and her son erected as heir apparent, Lady Li was dizzy with success. Years of machinations and intrigue had paid off at last. It seemed only a matter of time before she became empress.

At this critical juncture she made an irredeemable error. Emperor Jingdi's elder sister, titled Elder Princess, offered to marry her daughter, Ahjiao, to the heir apparent, Liu Rong.

In her opinion, close in age and equal in status, they would make a perfect couple. To her surprise and indignation, Lady Li flatly refused.

Lady Li, a jealous, short-sighted woman, regarded the other consorts with scorn and suspicion once she became the emperor's favorite. Because of her close relationship with the emperor, the Elder Princess was often asked by various consorts to speak to him in their favor. On several occasions, the princess brought some of the consorts to the emperor's attention. This infuriated Lady Li, who began to bear a biting hatred against the princess. That was why she turned down the marriage proposal without a moment's hesitation.

To divert herself, the Elder Princess paid Lady Wang a visit. At the mention of Ahjiao's marriage, the princess could hardly contain her anger. "I was doing her a favor by offering to marry my daughter to her son," she said. "She had absolutely no idea what is good for her!"

Lady Wang smiled blandly. "There is no need for you to brood over the matter. Please calm down, for anger may not be good for your health."

The princess, however, was still seething with indignation. "After Empress Bo was deposed, it occurred to me that I could ask His Majesty to make her the new empress, since he was obviously so fond of her. I didn't expect her to be so unreasonable! How can we allow a woman like her to preside over the rear palace?"

"It's really strange," said Lady Wang, "for her to disagree to such a perfect match. Ahjiao is such a bright and lovely child; no one could be a more suitable bride for the crown prince. Unfortunately my son is no crown prince. Otherwise he would be fortunate to have such a peerless maiden for his wife." She assumed a melancholy expression and threw a furtive glance at the princess.

"The crown prince!" the Elder Princess muttered, as if remembering something. She raised her eyebrows and twitched her mouth contemptuously. "It's not uncommon for a crown prince to be replaced! Li seems to regard herself as the empress just because her son is designated the crown prince. As long as I am breathing, her son will have no chance to wear the crown!"

Lady Wang tried hard to conceal her exultation. "Replacement of the crown prince is a matter of great importance to the state," she said seriously. "It does not seem appropriate for you to concern yourself with such things."

"I can do as I please," the princess rejoined. "Since she does not know how to appreciate a favor, I don't have to bear her interests in mind." Then an idea occurred to her. "I just thought of something," she told Lady Wang. "Why don't I marry my daughter to your son? Though she is a few years older, that shouldn't be a problem."

Lady Wang was delighted. "That would be wonderful!" she exclaimed, her face brightening up with a smile. "That would be more than I could ever wish for! But I doubt if my humble son is worthy of Ahjiao."

"If you don't object, the matter is settled," announced the Elder Princess. Feeling much better, she broke into a smile. "We will soon be in-laws!" The two women laughed heartily together.

Shortly afterward the marriage was settled with Emperor Jingdi's approval. Naturally, the Elder Princess and Lady Wang became intimate friends. Motivated by hatred or by craving for power, they worked hand in glove against Lady Li.

Lady Li Falls out of Favor

According to a rumor that spread quickly in the palace grounds, Lady Li cursed all the other consorts behind their backs and even employed witchcraft to harm them. The Elder Princess made a few unfavorable remarks about her to Emperor Jingdi. "Li is so narrow-minded and intolerant," she complained. "Due to jealousy and hatred, she is especially vicious to Lady Wang and often curses her. If such a person should become the empress one day, she would surely make a 'pig-woman' of her enemy!"

Emperor Jingdi felt a cold shudder running down his spine, for he was well acquainted with the story of Lady Qi, Emperor Gaozu's favorite consort. After his death the empress, Lü Zhi, had Lady Qi's limbs cut off. She was thrown into a manure pit and named "the pig-woman." Thus the words of his elder sister made a deep impression on Emperor Jingdi.

One day Emperor Jingdi took a stroll in the palace. He was not in high spirits, for he had just caught a cold, and his mind was burdened by the problems of the court. Arriving at Lady Li's residence, he remarked to her, "When I am gone, you must take good care of all my children. On no account should you forget this."

Lady Li pursed her lips, not saying anything, but there was a discontented look on her face. "What's wrong with you?" the emperor demanded irritably.

"I am not a nurse," said Lady Li irreverently. "Each prince has his own mother. Why should I be the one to look after them?"

Emperor Jingdi said nothing but walked away in great anger. She was indeed a narrow-minded woman, he told himself. He began to believe the rumors spread against her, and the prospect of her making a pig-woman of her enemy did not seem improbable. After this, his infatuation with Lady Li died quickly, and he began to consider deposing the heir apparent.

By her foolishly wayward manners, Lady Li missed her chance to impress her imperial master favorably. With the Elder Princess and Lady Wang constantly praising Liu Che for his intelligence, filial devotion, and personal grace, Emperor Jingdi could not remain unmoved. In the meantime Lady Wang tried her best to win the emperor's good graces by her tenderness, solicitude, modesty and obedience. To other palace women she was friendly and helpful, doling out small favors to obtain their support. In this way she managed to establish a good name for herself in the palace. Lady Li and her son, the heir apparent, dwindled rapidly in the emperor's estimation.

Ambition Fulfilled

A year passed with constant internecine strife in the imperial harem.

One day the minister in charge of rites presented a memorial asking Emperor Jingdi to make Lady Li his empress, on the ground that her son was already the heir apparent. The emperor, however, had long lost interest in Lady Li and her son, Liu Rong. Suspecting that Lady Li was maneuvering behind the scene, he burst into a wild fury. The minister was thrown into prison, and Liu Rong was demoted to Prince of Linjiang.

The emperor's decision caused a tumult in the court. Several ministers raised objections, but the emperor was too angry to listen to anyone.

Emperor Jingdi's suspicion of Lady Li was actually unfounded. It was Lady Wang who had sent her followers to talk the minister into presenting the fatal memorial, fully aware of how the emperor would react. Her plan met with total success. After the deposal of the heir apparent, Lady Li was no longer able to see the emperor. Crushed with sorrow and grief, she died soon afterwards of a broken heart. Liu Rong was then accused of the felony of expanding his residence by encroaching on the grounds of the imperial temples. He ended up hanging himself in prison.

In 149 B.C. Emperor Jingdi made Lady Wang empress, and her son, Liu Che, the crown prince. Lady Wang's dream came true at last. Thanks to her ingratiating wiles, secret maneuvers, and the ability to take quick action, this woman with one of the most obscure origins achieved the seemingly impossible: she became empress by her second marriage.

Lady Wang's triumph in the imperial harem not only changed her life but also affected the fate of the empire. Her son, the well-known Emperor Wudi of Han, ushered in a new era in the history of the Han Dynasty.

THE VICISSITUDES OF AHJIAO

Ahjiao was the daughter of the Elder Princess, Emperor Jingdi's elder sister. Liu Che, who later became Emperor Wudi of Han, was the ninth son of Emperor Jingdi by Lady Wang. Therefore Ahjiao and Liu Che were cousins.

In his childhood Liu Che often had Ahjiao for a playmate. His elevation at the age of three as Prince of Jiaodong did not affect his friendship with her.

One day the Elder Princess entered the palace with Ahjiao and found Liu Che playing by his mother's side. The Elder Princess put him on her knees, stroked his head, and said jokingly, "Little Che, do you want to get married?"

Liu Che grimaced for a reply. Pointing to an attending maid, the princess asked him, "Do you want her for a wife?"

"No!" Liu Che answered crisply, filling the room with laughter. The princess then pointed to Ahjiao and repeated the same question. Gazing at his lovely cousin, Liu Che broke into a big smile and announced solemnly, "If Ahjiao marries me, I will let her live in a house of gold."

Delighted, the Elder Princess took the boy into her arms and went to see her brother, Emperor Jingdi. After listening to the story, the emperor smiled and turned to question the boy, who repeated his announcement. Impressed, the emperor told himself that the two children might be meant for each other, and so he raised no objection to the match. Liu Che's mother, Lady Wang, also agreed with alacrity to the marriage.

After that the Elder Princess, for the sake of her daughter, often spoke favorably of Liu Che to the emperor. In the meantime Lady Wang succeeded in making herself the emperor's favorite. Thus Liu Che was set up as the heir apparent at the age of six and ascended the throne at age sixteen. He

reigned from 139 to 85 B.C.

At fourteen Ahjiao married Liu Che, who was then the crown prince, and after his ascension to the throne, Ahjiao became the empress. The young couple, passionately in love, spent a blissful time together. However, after ten years of marriage, Ahjiao remained childless. The Elder Princess grew worried, for the only way for Ahjiao to consolidate her position was to give birth to an imperial heir. To cure her daughter of sterility the princess resorted to medicine, divination and prayer, but in vain. Predictably, Emperor Wudi's fascination with Ahjiao began to wane.

One day Emperor Wudi visited his elder sister, who gave a feast to his honor and sent a team of beauties to wait on him. Emperor Wudi, seated by the fire, sat down to the food and wine with relish, showing no interest in the girls.

At this the princess beckoned an attendant. After a moment, a young maiden of stunning beauty walked into the hall and proceeded to sing in a sweet, melodious voice.

Emperor Wudi was at once enthralled by the girl. This did not escape the notice of his elder sister, who persuaded him to take her to the imperial palace with him. The girl, named Wei Zifu, later replaced Ahjiao as Liu Che's empress.

Wei Zifu's entry into the palace filled Ahjiao with consternation. She found the newcomer a serious threat to her supremacy in the rear palace. However, her efforts to weaken Wei Zifu's influence proved futile, for the emperor grew more and more enamored of her.

Ahjiao was thus superseded by Wei Zifu as the emperor's favorite. After giving birth to three daughters successively but no sons, Wei Zifu grew a bit worried, but there was hope as long as the emperor spent his nights almost exclusively in her company. Finally she gave birth to a son, who was named Liu Ju.

In the meantime Ahjiao, the empress, sank into inconsolable sorrow. For ten years she had enjoyed the emperor's exclusive favor. Then another woman, a mere singing girl, came and took everything away from her. She felt a stab of pain whenever the emperor spent the night in Wei Zifu's chamber, and felt like dying whenever Wei bore him a child. She lost her appetite and could hardly sleep at night. Longing in vain for the emperor's arrival, she grew languid day by day.

One day Ahjiao received a woman in her palace who dabbled in necromancy. By her instruction, Ahjiao had a wooden figure of Wei Zifu carved and buried with a curse, hoping thereby to hasten the death of her archenemy. Shortly afterward, one of her attendants told the emperor about this in the hope of getting a reward. Emperor Wudi was furious. As witchcraft was strictly forbidden in the imperial palace, the empress had knowingly committed an offense. She lost her title of empress and had to move to the out-of-the-way Changmen palace.

Ahjiao sat by the palace gate all day, gazing with tearful eyes at the clouds until they turned purple in the evening glow. The grass in the meadow withered in the autumn, then turned green again the following spring, but her beauty and youth were being taken away with no chance of return. She did not resign to her fate but decided to win back the emperor's favor. It occurred to her that the emperor was very fond of the writings of Sima Xiangru, a most talented scholar. When he read Sima's descriptive prose for the first time, he mistook the author for an ancient man and expressed regret over his inability to meet such a genius in person. Informed that Sima Xiangru was actually his contemporary, the emperor went into rapture, and immediately summoned him to the court and made him a civil minister. Ahjiao recalled several occasions when the emperor spoke highly of Sima Xiangru's elegant prose. Perhaps with his help she could enjoy a rejuvenation like the grass in spring, she told herself. With a little help she might be able to bring the emperor back to her side.

Sending handsome gifts, Ahjiao invited Sima Xiangru to

the Changmen palace, where she recounted to him the misfortune that had befallen her and poured out her longings for the emperor. Moved to pity, Sima Xiangru composed an essay for her, "Woman at Changmen," a well-known masterpiece of classic Chinese literature. It portrayed a deserted woman longing for her man to change his mind and return to her. The essay went on to tell how from dawn till dusk and through long, lonely nights the woman remained in her cold chamber with nothing but utter grief for a companion. Late into the night, she gazed at the bright moon with tearful eyes. To relieve her sorrow she picked up the zither to play, but the music flowing from its strings only added to her melancholy and disillusion. It seemed that her sorrow, like the dark night, would never come to an end. Despite all this, in her heart there was still a glimmer of hope that one day her imperial master would return to her side.

On reading "Woman at Changmen" Emperor Wudi exclaimed in admiration. Unfortunately, he was impressed not so much by the deplorable fate of the abandoned woman as by the grace and elegance of the prose. He had no intention to rehabilitating the disgraced empress.

For a long time Ahjiao stood by the palace gate all day hoping to catch a glimpse of the emperor's chariot. By and by, hope turned to disappointment, then to despair. Her days of glory and happiness would never return. She spent the rest of her life in Changmen palace.

The Elder Princess had envisaged a bright future for Ahjiao by marrying her to the prospective emperor. Contrary to her expectation, Ahjiao proved a loser in the constant fight within the imperial harem and ended her life in misery and desolation.

THE "FIST LADY" LOSES HER LIFE

On a fine day Emperor Wudi left the capital for a hunting tour in Hejian. An attendant skilled at necromancy told him that there must be some unusual person living in the area judging by the auspicious clouds gathering in the sky. Intrigued, the emperor ordered the guards to make a search.

A moment later the guards brought back a very lovely girl. Apart from her shining visage, she did have something unusual about her: her hands were clasped into tight fists and she could not straighten her fingers.

Curious, the emperor walked up to her and stroked her hands gently. Gradually the girl extended her palms and began to move her fingers with facility. Pleased, the emperor took her with him and had the Gouyi palace built as her residence. Nicknamed the "Fist Lady," she joined the imperial harem at eighteen and became the last of Emperor Wudi's favorite consorts.

Later she gave birth to a son after a pregnancy of fourteen months. Pleased to have a son in his old age, the emperor named the baby Fuling. Once he remarked to some attendants, "The great King Yao took fourteen months to be born. Maybe Fuling has something in common with Yao!" After that he bestowed increasing favor on the Fist Lady and her son.

A few years later a bizarre incident took place in the palace. A suspicious-looking man wearing a sword was seen by Emperor Wudi to walk into the palace without permission. The guards conducted a thorough search but failed to find the man. The emperor considered this to be an ill omen.

In his later years Emperor Wudi became a sickly, irritable old man. He suspected that his illness was caused by witchcraft in the palace. At his order, the guards dug deeply into the palace grounds. They unearthed a wooden figurine, and a flurry of interrogation and torture followed. There was panic and confusion among the residents of the palace as more and more people became implicated in the witch hunt.

Then someone told Emperor Wudi that the heir apparent had made many wooden figures inscribed with vicious curses. The heir apparent went into panic and sought help from his mother, the empress. They decided to destroy the implicator by force. Emperor Wudi, informed that this was a revolt against him, commanded the troops to pacify the situation. The fight that ensued resulted in more than ten thousand casualties. Both the heir apparent and the empress ended by taking their own lives.

Not until a year later did Emperor Wudi learn to his remorse the truth behind the bloody turmoil. Overcome with regret, he began to feel very old. He did not have much more time to find an heir to whom he could entrust the Han empire.

One day Emperor Wudi was walking up and down in the Gouyi Palace when he caught sight of Fuling, then a seven-year-old boy. He was loveable, healthy and intelligent. It suddenly occurred to the emperor that this boy, like the great King Yao, had taken fourteen months to be born. Why not make him heir to the throne? Yet how could such a young boy reign in the court without interference? What if the boy was made a puppet, with his mother ruling the empire as Lü Zhi had done after Emperor Gaozu's demise? After much deliberation, Emperor Wudi made a chilling decision. He would get rid of the mother.

Shortly thereafter, on a day when the Fist Lady was attending to the emperor and smiling brightly, he remained sullen. Falling on her knees, she begged to know the reason of his displeasure. The emperor suddenly swore at her and ordered her to be taken out and executed. Terrified, she begged tearfully for mercy, hoping the emperor would pardon her on account of the many happy days they had shared. But the emperor only smiled coldly and hurled more abuses at her. The Fist Lady was thus executed. It was said that the sky became overcast with dust on that day.

Emperor Wudi asked his attendants what they thought of his decision. "We are puzzled," they replied. "Her Ladyship always served Your Majesty with devotion and never committed any offense. Besides, Your Majesty has just announced his intention to make her son the crown prince. Instead of being invited to a feast of celebration, she was put to death without cause. It is really beyond our understanding."

"Such a matter of vital significance is indeed beyond the understanding of ordinary people," Emperor Wudi said with a sigh. "With a child on the throne, his mother would be too young to live alone by herself. By her trespasses she would be liable to plunge the court into chaos and even bring the entire empire to the verge of collapse. Therefore, precisely because I intend to have Fuling for my successor, I cannot let his mother survive me."

Though he was able to rationalize his cruelty toward the Fist Lady, the emperor felt sorry for her and had the Tongyun Terrace built in her honor. A bird was said to visit the terrace every day until Fuling ascended to the throne.

EMPRESS MA DECLINES TO ELEVATE EXTERNAL RELATIVES

Emperor Mingdi (reigned 57-75) had Lady Ma as his empress. She was one of the most virtuous, talented, and diligent women ever to emerge from China's imperial harem.

Recommendation by Elder Brother

Lady Ma's father, Ma Yuan, was a meritorious general who died of illness during an expedition. After his death he was wrongly accused of hoarding plunder for personal use. This caused Liu Xiu, or Emperor Guangwudi of Han, to deprive Ma Yuan of his title as marquis. Actually, the so-called plunder was medicinal herbs, which Ma Yuan had bought at the frontier and brought back home in order to treat his arthritis, which he contracted during his military campaigns. When this fact was presented to the emperor, he conceded to the general's innocence. Nevertheless the power and prestige of the Ma family declined quickly.

Ma Yan, a nephew of the late general, decided to work to restore the family to its former glory. He wrote a memorial to recommend Ma Yuan's three daughters for the imperial harem, saying, "According to what I have heard, not enough consorts have been found for the heir apparent and other imperial princes. My late uncle, Ma Yuan, left three daughters, who are aged fifteen, fourteen and thirteen respectively. All of them are above average in terms of appearance. Besides, they are endowed with a gentle and modest disposition, good manners, and filial piety. I beseech Your Majesty to send an envoy to take a look at them. If any of them should be selected, my late uncle would feel much comforted in his

grave."

On reading this memorial, Emperor Guangwudi recalled Ma Yuan's numerous exploits and his subsequent disgrace on a trumped-up charge. The head eunuch was sent to visit the Ma family and he chose the youngest of the three girls. Upon entry into the palace she was allocated to be a consort for the heir apparent.

At thirteen the girl was already carrying out her household duties with the diligence, consideration, and modesty of an adult. She soon won the hearts of other consorts in the palace by her warmth, earnestness, and civility. The attending maids also liked her for her unusual tolerance and tenderness. To the empress she was humble, modest, and solicitous, displaying an excellent upbringing. The crown prince became greatly enamored of her.

Entering the palace as a young maiden, Ma reached womanhood a few years later, with her beauty in full bloom. She was of a medium height, with a slender figure, a rosy face with red lips always on the verge of a smile, and a pair of large, bright eyes as pure as a crystal clear pool in autumn. Especially attractive was her glossy black hair which she combed into a big bun. Despite the unusual favor bestowed on her by the crown prince, she showed no sign of arrogance or jealousy and treated everyone with proper courtesy. It seemed even then that she was fit to be an empress.

When Emperor Guangwudi died of illness at the age of sixty-two, the crown prince, Liu Zhuang, succeeded him to the throne. He became known as Emperor Mingdi. Upon Liu Zhuang's ascension, Ma received the title of Worthy Lady. Three years later she was made empress.

A Paragon of Virtue in the Rear Palace

Lady Ma had no child of her own. "If a woman cannot bear her own child," she once remarked, "Why can't she bring up a foster child like her own?" Such openmindedness and generosity was in sharp contrast with the renowned Zhao sisters, consorts of the late Emperor Chengdi. Both of them were sterile, so they were green with envy against any palace woman who got pregnant or gave birth. They either forced the pregnant woman to have an abortion or put her new-born baby to death. As a result Emperor Chengdi died with no child of his own to succeed to the throne.

Lady Ma treated the children of the emperor's consorts with great tenderness and solicitude. One of them, Lady Jia, gave birth to a son named Liu Da. Lady Ma brought up this child with the utmost care and treated him like her own. After she became empress, Liu Da was set up as the crown prince in the same year.

Her education partly accounted for Lady Ma's exemplary conduct. She was conversant with classic literature such as *The Book of Changes, The Spring and Autumn Annals,* presumably edicted by Confucius, poems by the great Chu poet Qu Yuan and works by Dong Zhongshu, a famous Confucian scholar. Because of her beauty, talent and virtuousness she gained universal respect in the imperial palace.

As stipulated by palace rules, the empress and the consorts were expected to pay their respect to the emperor on the first and fifteenth day of each month. On one occasion the consorts, dressed in their best attire, found Lady Ma in a coarsely knit robe, so they speculated that it must be made of the best cloth. On closer scrutiny, however, they found it to be a laceless dress made of coarse, thick silk. Some of them could not help snickering.

With a glance Lady Ma realized the cause of their amusement, but she did not take offense. "This coarse silk dyes very easily," she explained, "so I prefer to have my clothes made of it. There is nothing funny about this." The consorts fell silent, filled with wonder and respect.

Lady Ma displayed her talents and fairness in dealing with the daily affairs in the rear palace. On several occasions

Emperor Mingdi asked her to read and comment on memorials presented by his ministers. Much to his admiration, Lady Ma always came up with a sound solution to each problem quickly.

Emperor Mingdi was very fond of feasts and excursions. Lady Ma often advised him to cut down on such extravagances as they might interfere with his regal duties and impair his health. One sunny day the emperor decided to take his consorts with him on an excursion. The consorts, delighted to enjoy a respite from the monotony of their secluded life, soon arrived from various quarters of the palace. However, Lady Ma did not show up. When some consorts suggested inviting the empress, the emperor said with a smile, "She has no taste for pleasure and would not be happy should we invite her to come. Let us leave her alone!"

When Lady Ma learned of the excursion, she did not get angry. From then on she offered her advice more tactfully. Whenever the emperor was to take an outing, she would decline to come by pleading poor health. By and by the emperor no longer invited her on such occasions.

Declining to Elevate External Relatives

By the eighteenth year of the Yongping reign under Emperor Mingdi (75) the empire had enjoyed over five decades of peace. Because of such long-time social stability, there was a marked growth in production and improvement in the people's livelihood. A favorable climate gave the peasants yet another bumper harvest that year.

But it was also in this year that Emperor Mingdi died. Liu Da, Lady Ma's foster son, succeeded to the throne, to be known as Emperor Zhangdi. Thereupon Lady Ma received the title of empress dowager.

During Emperor Mingdi's reign Lady Ma had repeatedly declined promotion and rewards for her family members. When Emperor Mingdi made a list of twenty-eight meritorious generals and had their portraits painted, Ma Yuan was not included because of Lady Ma's objection. In her opinion, though her father had achieved great merits and had been implicated in a false charge, the case had been subsequently cleared, so there was no more need to confer further honors on him. Because of her attitude none of her three brothers, who served as low-ranking officials in the court, received any promotion during Mingdi's reign.

Upon his ascension Emperor Zhangdi immediately promoted Lady Ma's brothers, whom he regarded as his uncles, to high posts. The Ma brothers thus became powerful personages in the imperial court, and many ministers swarmed around them to curry their favor. But a few officials sent memorials to the emperor advising him against giving "external relatives," or relatives of the emperor on his wife's or mother's side, high posts or special rewards. Unmoved, Emperor Zhangdi decided to elevate his uncles as marquises. However, he was compelled to put the matter on the shelf when Lady Ma raised a strong objection.

The following year the empire suffered a severe drought. At this, some sycophantic courtiers presented memorials blaming the disaster on the emperor's failure to elevate his external relatives. Emperor Zhangdi was ready to agree, but again the empress dowager stopped him. She issued an edict to the court officials, pointing out that those who sent in their memorials requesting the elevation of external relatives were merely trying to win the favor of the emperor for their own benefit. She cited many historical events that proved the dire consequences of an emperor's partiality toward his external relatives. "As the imperial mother of all under heaven," she said, "I desire no more than enough food and clothing for all my subjects. For myself, I am content enough to wear coarse clothes and eat simple meals. I also require my attendants to practice parsimony in the hope of setting a good example for others." Only thus, she said, could she adhere to the instruction of the late emperor, do justice to the virtues of her ancestors, and avoid reenacting the tragedies in history.

After the edict was proclaimed, no courtier dared take up the topic again. Emperor Zhangdi, though deeply touched, did not change his mind. He pleaded with Lady Ma, saying, "Since the establishment of the Han empire, it has been customary to make imperial sons princes and imperial uncles marquises. Your modesty, though highly commendable, has prevented your son from elevating his three uncles! They are either advanced in years or suffering from illness. If anything untoward should happen to them before they receive the titles they fully deserve, I would bear everlasting regret. There should be no more delay over the matter!"

"How can you blame my modesty for preventing you from elevating your uncles?" retorted Lady Ma. "After careful consideration, I think it is unsuitable to elevate them. Formerly, Emperor Gaozu made it a rule that anyone who has not achieved military exploits shall not be entitled to a fiefdom. Your uncles have not achieved any merits for the empire, so they do not deserve to be elevated. A high position and handsome salary corrupts a man just like an injury to the roots impairs the life of a tree. When someone with enough to eat and wear and leave to posterity still hankers after elevation, isn't it a matter of greed? A filial child should be content when his relatives are living in peace and security. Moreover, the empire has been inflicted with one calamity after another, and the price of grain has risen sharply. Why not focus your attention on this problem? In the future, when the balance of yin and yang is restored in the empire and it becomes free of natural disasters or troubles along the border, I will devote my attention to my grandchildren and bother no more about state affairs!"

Lady Ma then issued another edict stipulating that if anyone from the Ma family should commit an offense, the officials concerned should report the matter to the court without fail. When she learned that the height of her mother's grave exceeded the specified limit, she immediately told her brothers to reduce it. At her order, all members of the Ma family received rewards or punishments in strict accordance with their merits or misdeeds.

Two years later the empire enjoyed a bumper harvest and was free of border conflicts. Therefore Emperor Jingdi elevated his three uncles without consulting the empress dowager first. At this Lady Ma heaved a deep sigh. "When young, I was ready to give up my life to earn a good name. In my old age, I try to abide by ancient precepts and guard against greed. I live a simple life and pay no attention to luxuries, so that I can be worthy of the late emperor. For the best interests of the state, I tried my best to keep my brothers from getting noble titles, but to no avail. This will be a lifelong regret for me!"

On learning of her attitude, her three brothers all handed in memorials declining their elevations. When the emperor insisted on promoting them, they accepted the titles but resigned from their official posts, leaving the imperial court for their respective fiefs.

DENG SUI, A LEARNED, KINDLY EMPRESS

Deng Sui was the empress of Emperor Hedi of Han (reigned 88-105). As a child she was intelligent and considerate. Once, her grandmother decided to give her a haircut. Due to poor eyesight, the old woman hurt Deng's head with the scissors, but the five-year-old girl bore the pain without uttering a sound until her grandmother finished. "Didn't it hurt?" she was asked afterward. "Why didn't you cry?"

"Of course it hurt," the little girl replied. "But Grandma gave me the haircut because she loves me so much. If I cried out in pain, I would hurt her feelings. That's why I didn't cry." The words of the small child filled the listeners with wonder.

Deng Sui began studying ancient classics at the age of six. Sometimes she posed questions to her elder brothers, who did not always knew the answer. Thus she gained the nickname Young Scholar in the family.

Devoted to book learning, Deng Sui showed little interest in the affairs of the household. Her mother began to grow anxious. "Why are you reading all day without learning to do any needlework? Do you think you can read books all your life? Someday you will get married and have household duties to attend to."

Deng Sui, a filial child, did not want to disobey her mother's instructions. Neither did she want to give up reading. So she began to do needlework during the day and stayed up late at night reading books. Her father was quite fond of her. When he died, Deng Sui wore mourning for him for three years, during which time she grew emaciated because of fasting.

Soon afterward Deng Sui became one of the many beautiful maidens chosen to enter the palace. Not knowing if this bade good or ill, the family consulted a necromancer, who marveled at her unusual visage. After learning something about the girl, he became convinced of her good fortune. "The young maiden has a noble face," he declared. "Someday she will become an imperial consort."

Before Deng Sui left home, her mother admonished her to conduct herself with caution and meticulously abide by the palace rules. "Your fate is in your own hands," she warned. Upon her entry into the palace, Deng Sui got the title Worthy Lady. She did not became the emperor's favorite overnight. Another Worthy Lady named Yin, who had entered the palace three years earlier, commanded the emperor's full attention. Apart from her good looks, she was intelligent and full of womanly charms. Shortly after Deng Sui's entry into the palace, Lady Yin was made empress.

The emperor then became more and more fascinated by Deng Sui. She was taller than the empress, and the grace and elegance with which she conducted herself attested to her perfect upbringing. With her quiet courtesy and gentle manners, she possessed a unique charm that gripped the heart of the emperor. He began to frequent her residence.

The empress burned with jealousy. One day, when the emperor was enjoying a feast with his empress and his consorts, Lady Yin suddenly remarked, "Look at Worthy Lady Deng! What a magnificently tall figure she has! Doesn't she look like a crane standing among chickens?" Deng Sui threw herself on the ground, saying, "I owe my humble looks to my parents, and now I owe everything I have to the kindness of the empress. Please take pity on me!" Her sincere and modest attitude left the empress with no excuse to go on with her tirade. Deng Sui soon gained universal respect among the palace women. Bearing in mind her mother's admonition, she watched her steps with the utmost caution and never failed to treat the empress with due respect and submission.

Generous in disposition, Deng Sui not only treated other consorts with sincerity and modesty, but showed concern and kindness toward the attendants and palace maids. Once, when she fell ill, Emperor Hedi gave special permission for her mother and brother to visit her in the palace for an indefinite period of time. Deng Sui declined the emperor's offer, saying, "If my family members are allowed to stay in the forbidden grounds of the palace, the court officials will blame Your Majesty for his partiality, and I would also be criticized. This would cause inconvenience both at the court and in the rear palace." Her reply increased Emperor Hedi's regard for her.

Because of his growing infatuation with Deng Sui, the emperor began to treat his empress with indifference. Deng Sui became anxious about this. When the emperor came to spend the night with her, she often tried to excuse herself, saying she was not feeling well, so that he could enjoy the company of his empress or other consorts. Unlike the other women of the palace, Lady Yin remained unmoved by Deng Sui's courtesy and generous manners.

Once, when Emperor Hedi took to his bed with a serious illness, Lady Yin muttered to her attendants, "When I can do what I please, I will wipe out the Deng family! She has only a few days left to give herself airs!" Informed of the empress' remark, Deng Sui was dumbfounded. "All my humility and obedience to the empress have been in vain!" she cried in bitter tears. Then to prevent her family from being implicated, she decided to kill herself. But when she was about to drink poison, one of the maids brought her a false message that the emperor had recovered and expressed his intention to see her. Hearing this, Deng Sui knelt in gratitude to pay homage to heaven and earth. The next day the emperor did have a miraculous recovery.

Her jealousy growing with each passing day, Lady Yin asked her grandmother to employ witchcraft against Deng Sui.

When this plot was uncovered, Emperor Hedi was furious. Lady Yin was deprived of her title and sent to live in a remote part of the palace, where she died of melancholy a year later.

Soon after Lady Yin's deposal, Deng Sui was made empress at the age of twenty-two. She immediately stopped the court from receiving precious gifts from local officials, only accepting books, writing brushes and ink slabs. To better her education she appointed a few talented women to be her tutors.

Two years later Emperor Hedi died, and Deng Sui, now the empress dowager, presided over the court. For ten years she ruled the Han empire with diligence and benevolence, pacifying internal turmoils and external disturbances. She prevented her family members from appropriating state power for their private benefit. Under her auspices, a school was set up for imperial children of both sexes above the age of five. This was probably the first mixed school in China.

Deng Sui died of illness at the age of forty-one.

JIA NANFENG,
AN UGLY AND VICIOUS EMPRESS

Emperor Huidi (reigned 289-306) of the Western Jin Dynasty had an unusually cruel and ferocious woman, Jia Nanfeng, for his empress. Because of his ineptness, Jia Nanfeng wielded imperial power to her heart's content, bringing about not only her own death but also the collapse of the dynasty.

The Ugly Girl Is Chosen

Though his eldest son, Sima Yan, was a moron, Emperor Wudi made him the crown prince. When he announced his intention to select a wife for this twelve-year-old prince, a fierce contention ensued in the imperial palace.

Emperor Wudi had his eyes on the daughter of Chief General Wei Guan. The news plunged another general, Jia Cong, and his wife, Guo Huai, into great disappointment and anxiety, for they were keen on marrying their own daughter to the crown prince.

Guo Huai was an excessively jealous and cruel woman. On one occasion, when the wet nurse had her own son in her arms, Jia Cong stroked the baby's face with his hand. Seeing this, Guo Huai became convinced that the wet nurse was her husband's secret lover and had her flogged to death.

When planning for her daughter's future, Guo Huai remembered the saying that "money can buy a god's service." So she bribed some palace women to speak in favor of her daughter to the empress, Lady Yang.

When Emperor Wudi returned from an audience one day, Empress Yang said to him, "Jia Cong's daughter has both virtue and talent. She is fit to be the princess-consort for the crown prince."

"No, not at all," responded the emperor, shaking his head emphatically.

"Why not?" the empress asked in surprise.

"I want to have Wei Guan's daughter for my son's wife," the emperor explained. "Wei Guan is an honest man with a big, prosperous family. His daughter is tall, white-skinned, and pretty. As for Jia Cong, he has had few children by that jealous wife of his. His daughter is short and dark-skinned. Why should I choose stone over jade?"

Empress Yang was puzzled at the disparity between the emperor's opinion and what she had been told. After a pause, she said, "Can't Your Majesty change his mind? With her virtue and talent, Jia Cong's daughter is the most suitable one to be our future daughter-in-law." When the emperor did not answer, she suggested, "Why not consult your ministers about the matter? Ask them which girl is better." She knew that Jia Cong had great influence in the court, and most officials would speak in his favor. Emperor Wudi nodded his assent.

The following day the emperor gave a feast to some court officials in the rear palace. When he asked their opinion about the suitable candidate for the crown prince's bride, a minister named Xun Mao spoke first, lavishing praise on Jia Cong's daughter. Several ministers eagerly agreed with his opinion. Puzzled, the emperor began to doubt his own judgement. "How many daughters does Jia Cong have?" he asked.

"Jia Cong has had two daughters by his first wife, and both are married. His daughters by his present wife are young maidens who are not engaged."

"How old are these two girls?"

"The younger one, aged eleven, is prettier. She can be the princess-consort."

"Eleven is too young," the emperor said.

"The elder one is aged fourteen," continued Xun Mao hastily. "Though not as pretty as her younger sister, she is superior in virtue and talent. The worthiness of a woman should be judged by her virtue rather than her appearance. I beseech Your Majesty to give the matter due consideration!"

Emperor Wudi finally gave in. "All right," he said. "The crown prince will have Jia Cong's third daughter for his wife." Hearing this, all the ministers rose from their seats to offer their congratulations. They drank a lot of wine and took their leave in high spirits. Xun Mao went straight to the Jia family to report the good news.

A year later the crown prince married Jia Cong's third daughter, Jia Nanfeng. She was stodgy and dark-skinned, and had ungainly moles behind her eyebrows. Only then did Emperor Wudi realize his mistake, but it was too late to make amends.

Murder of the Empress Dowager

In 290 Emperor Wudi of Jin died. The crown prince, Sima Zhong, ascended the throne, to be known as Emperor Huidi. Jia Nanfeng was elevated to empress. Yang Zhi, Emperor Wudi's second empress, received the title of empress dowager. But the most powerful person in the imperial court was Chief Minister Yang Jun, father-in-law of the late Emperor Wudi.

Despite her exalted position, Empress Jia was far from happy. Yang Jun's arrogance and lack of scruples was a constant irritation to her. Among court officials he was the only one who refused to come to the main hall of the palace to bid farewell to Emperor Wudi's remains. To win public support for himself, he gave promotions to all the officials and functionaries in the empire, despite the objections of the other ministers. "One of these days the old scoundrel will get his due!" Jia Nanfeng cursed fiercely.

Another seeming injustice she could not bear was her duty to wait on Yang Zhi, the empress dowager, who was two years her junior. She still chafed over an embarassing, but minor incident that had taken place when she was the princess-consort, and Yang Zhi the empress. Because she had several daughters but no son, Jia Nanfeng was envious when one of the prince's consorts, Xie Mei, bore him a son. After that she could not bear to have any consort become pregnant. She even struck a pregnant consort with a halberd, causing the woman to die of a miscarriage. Emperor Wudi would have deposed her but for the intervention of Empress Yang, who argued that the princess-consort would certainly mend her ways when she grew older and more sensible. Instead of showing her gratitude, Jia Nanfeng became even more aversive to Empress Yang.

Jia Nanfeng thought about the balance of power in the court. Though most courtiers held Yang Jun in awe, they were not necessarily his willing followers. Meng Guan and Li Zhao, for instance, were both hostile to Yang Jun, while a few princes of the Sima family were also dissatisfied with Yang's monopoly of power. Besides, she had some cohorts of her own, such as Dong Meng, a palace attendant.

She summoned Li Zhao for a secret meeting, and sent him out to test the water for her. A few days later he reported to her that Sima Liang, the Prince of Runan, was overcautious and dared not stage a coup. Sima Wei, the twenty-one-year-old Prince of Chu, however, offered to take concerted action with her to wipe out Yang Jun and his followers. Jia Nanfeng instructed her cohorts to get ready for the big action.

Shortly afterward Sima Wei submitted a memorial requesting that he be transferred back to the imperial capital. Yang Jun had often worried that Sima Wei, an undisciplined man in command of a formidable force, would make trouble in his fief, and was therefore glad to have him back in the capital, where he could be subjected to close supervision. His request granted, Sima Wei arrived in the capital some days later, accompanied by Sima Yun, the Prince of Huainan.

Emperor Huidi is one of the better-known feeble-minded rulers in Chinese history. When he was touring the imperial garden one day he heard frogs croaking and, turning to his attendants, asked, "Are those official or private frogs?" A quick-witted attendant replied, "Those that croak in the imperial garden must be official frogs, and those that croak in privately-owned rice fields would be private ones." The emperor nodded his agreement and praised the attendant for his sound knowledge. On another occasion he was informed that a natural calamity had resulted in the starvation of many people. "Why were these people so stupid?" he demanded. "Why didn't they eat meat porridge?" It was too much to expect such an emperor to make a sound judgement on anything. So when Meng Guan and Li Zhao, following Jia Nanfeng's instructions, went to see the emperor one night to accuse Yang Jun of plotting a revolt, the emperor immediately ordered Sima Wei to lay siege to the Chief Minister's residence.

Despite his arrogance and overbearing manner Yang Jun lacked the ability to deal with emergencies. He was on tenterhooks, not knowing what to do. Instead of attempting to save the situation, his followers deserted him at the critical moment.

The empress dowager, Yang Zhi, was overwhelmed by fear. In an attempt to help her father, she took a piece of silk and wrote a few words on it, offering a high reward to anyone who could save the Chief Minister. Then she had the silk tied to an arrow which was shot out of the palace. Unfortunately it was picked up by one of Jia Nanfeng's attendants. "The empress dowager has joined her father in the revolt!" she announced. "Anyone who follows her orders will be put to death!"

The soldiers first set Yang Jun's residence on fire, then stormed in, killing everyone they met. When they went to the horseshed, they found there was a man trembling inside. With a loud shout they commanded him to come out and surrender himself, but the man did not move. Losing their tempers, the soldiers speared through the shed. The man uttered a shrill cry and dropped dead on a heap of manure. Taken out of the shed, he was identified as Yang Jun.

Following Yang Jun's death, his followers and family members were massacred. The death toll ran to several thousand. When the carnage was over, Jia Nanfeng declared, "Yang Jun's wife deserves to be beheaded along with him. However, since she is the empress dowager's mother, she will be spared and sent to live with her daughter." Thus the empress dowager, Yang Zhi, and her mother were put under house arrest in the Yongning palace.

Shortly afterward, Jia Nanfeng maneuvered a few ministers into making accusations against the empress dowager, claiming her to be Yang Jun's accomplice in the revolt. After a fierce debate in court, Yang Zhi was deposed and demoted to the rank of a commoner.

After that, another memorial was submitted arguing that Yang Jun's wife, Lady Pang, should be beheaded. Since she had been spared for the sake of her daughter, now that her daughter was no longer the empress dowager, there was no longer any reason to overlook her guilt. When some guards tied up the old woman and led her away, Yang Zhi burst into desperate wails. Prostrating herself before Jia Nanfeng, she began to kowtow nonstop, pleading mercy for her aged mother. But Jia Nanfeng remained unmoved.

Early the next year Jia Nanfeng ordered that all the attending maids be taken away from Yang Zhi. With nothing to eat and no way of escape, Yang Zhi starved to death by the end of eight days. For fear that her ghost would tell the story to the late Emperor Wudi, Jia Nanfeng ordered that her body to be buried in a prone position, with a magic spell placed on her back so she would never be able to get up in the underworld and complain to anyone.

Killing Two Birds with One Stone

With the elimination of Yang Jun and his followers, Sima

Liang now became the dominant figure in the imperial court. In the subsequent handing out of rewards, over a thousand military officials received noble titles. Both Sima Liang and Wei Guan, the powerful general, had a strong mistrust of Sima Wei, the Prince of Chu, who had displayed his valor and vindictiveness in the campaign against Yang Jun. They decided it would be too dangerous to let him stay on in the capital, so they planned to deprive him of his military command by sending him back to his fief.

Sima Wei, who considered himself a big hero, was unwilling to submit to such manipulation and consulted his advisors on a countermeasure. One of them suggested joining forces with Empress Jia to fight Sima Liang and Wei Guan.

Sima Wei's offer came at an opportune time. Jia Nanfeng was fuming over Sima Liang's monopoly of power in the court, and she had old scores to settle with Wei Guan, who had once advised Emperor Wudi to depose Sima Zhong, the crown prince. By allying herself with Sima Wei she could eliminate these two enemies. On the other hand, Jia Nanfeng did not trust Sima Wei either. She found him intransigent and unreliable. She vowed that after Sima Liang and Wei Guan had been removed, she would set out to dispatch Sima Wei.

Having worked out her plot, Jia Nanfeng called on Emperor Huidi to accuse Sima Liang and Wei Guan of plotting to depose him. At her dictation, the witless emperor immediately issued a secret edict. Early the next morning Jia Nanfeng had the edict taken to Sima Wei along with her suggestion that he strike without delay.

Opening the edict Sima Wei read the following: "Sima Liang and Wei Guan have committed high treason by plotting to depose the emperor. You shall proclaim this edict, deploy the troops to guard the palace gates and deprive the two traitors of their posts and titles." Sima Wei hesitated for a moment, knowing the edict must have been cooked up by Empress Jia. Then he decided to go ahead, thinking he would become the most powerful man in the court after the purge of Sima Liang and Wei Guan.

Believing he had nothing to fear, Sima Wei declared that he had been mandated to command the imperial troops both in and outside the court. He dispatched Li Zhao to storm Sima Liang's residence, and dispatched Sima Xia, the Prince of Qinghe, to seize General Wei Guan.

After breakfast Sima Liang was about to leave for the palace when a tumult broke out outside his house. Before he could react, Li Zhao burst in with the troops and had him tied up, dragged out, and thrown on the ground beside a carriage. Li Zhao and his men then went on to hunt down and slaughter Sima Liang's family members. It was a sultry day in summer. Sima Liang, who was very fat, soon became drenched in sweat. A soldier took pity on him and began to fan him. Li Zhao was walking out of the house when he saw this. For fear that his followers would come to Sima Liang's rescue, he called out, "Whoever kills Sima Liang will be rewarded with a thousand bundles of cloth!" Many soldiers rushed over with swords, axes and other weapons. Sima Liang was cut into pieces instantly.

In the meantime Sima Xia had the residence of Wei Guan surrounded. At his order some soldiers shouted at the gate, "His Majesty has ordered Wei Guan to come out and receive punishment for his guilt!" With no way of escape, Wei Guan walked out and saluted Sima Xia. "I am willing to accompany you to meet His Majesty. Please have mercy and spare my family." Before Sima Xia could say another word, a man standing behind him leapt forward and, with a sweep of his broadsword, sliced Wei Guan in two. Everyone stared in amazement. This turned out to be Rong Hui, a petty officer of the imperial guards. A former servant in Wei Guan's house, he had been beaten severely and driven out because of some minor offense. Now, at last, he had the chance to take his revenge. After killing Wei Guan, he stormed into the house and went on a rampage. Wei Guan's entire family, including his three sons, six grandsons and over a hundred women, were all slaughtered.

With the two leading ministers killed by Sima Wei, the imperial court became overcast with fear and apprehension, every official worrying for his own safety. Zhang Hua had a message delivered to Jia Nanfeng, saying, "The Prince of Chu has arrogated imperial power by eliminating Sima Liang and Wei Guan. How can the emperor and empress enjoy their peace after that?" Delighted, Jia Nanfeng decided to employ Zhang Hua to execute her plan.

With little difficulty Jia Nanfeng and Zhang Hua persuaded the emperor to issue another edict denouncing Sima Wei for "executing court officials without authorization." Wang Gong, an officer of the imperial guards, was dispatched to arrest Sima Wei. Arriving at the Prince of Chu's residence, Wang Gong announced, "The Prince of Chu fabricated an imperial edict and executed court officials without authorization. He must be punished for such heinous offences. I have His Majesty's order to apprehend him, and anyone who dares to assist him will be decapitated on the spot!"

Sima Wei's guards and servants fled for their lives in all directions. A moment later there was only Sima Wei and his carriage driver left in the house.

Before his execution Sima Wei brought out the secret edict to plead his innocence. "I have acted at His Majesty's order," he cried out. "How can you charge me of killing court officials without authorization?" The officer in charge of the execution, aware of his innocence, nevertheless carried out his duties without question. Upon Sima Wei's death, Jia Nanfeng went on to redress the cases against Sima Liang and Wei Guan. However, neither of them had a single relative left by that time.

By one bloody case after another, Jia Nanfeng eliminated almost all of her enemies until imperial power was firmly grasped in her own hands.

Deposal of the Crown Prince

With most of the powerful figures of the imperial family eliminated, Jia Nanfeng found her next target in the crown prince, Sima Yu, who would surely challenge her authority when he came of age.

Sima Yu's mother was a palace woman named Xie Mei. When he became the crown prince, Xie Mei received the title Lady of Virtue. As a boy Sima Yu was bright and quick-witted. Emperor Wudi placed high hopes on him, expecting him to become a capable ruler. But as he grew up, he lost interest in studies and devoted all his time to merrymaking in the company of his consorts and palace maids.

Jia Nanfeng, who had been jealous of the crown prince's intelligence, found his degeneration very pleasing and highly desirable. If he should create some big trouble one day, that would give her a good reason to depose him. Thus she secretly encouraged him to fool around and indulge in his orgies and debauchery. Sima Yu set up a wineshop and meatshop on the palace grounds and became a very adept clerk, capable of telling the exact amount of wine or meat by a glance. He had vegetables and fowls produced in the imperial garden and taken out for sale in the market. With the money from such sales he either went on a spending spree or handed out rewards to his servants. He turned a deaf ear to those who tried to persuade him to mend his ways.

Jia Nanfeng had a nephew named Jia Mi, who was her right-hand man in all her misdeeds. A childhood companion of the crown prince, he was sly and artful. On instructions from his aunt, he spent his days in the company of the crown prince, aiding and abetting the crown price in all his low-down pursuits.

Jia Nanfeng, who had remained childless until then, suddenly announced her pregnancy. Later she gave birth to a baby boy, who was named Weizu. News of the empress having given birth to an imperial heir circulated in the palace at lightening speed and soon became known to the public at large. Actually, the baby was borne to the empress's younger sister, Jia Wu, but Jia Nanfeng claimed the child for her own with an eye to substituting him for Sima Yu.

One evening Sima Yu received a summons to enter the palace to see the emperor, who was said to be suffering from a sudden illness. Braving the cold weather, he arrived at his father's residence. At the front hall he was stopped by a palace maid holding a dish of fresh dates and a pot of wine. "On account of the cold weather, His Majesty has awarded you fresh dates and warm wine. You can have them before you go in."

"I never drink," said the crown prince. "Let me skip the wine."

"Are you afraid that the wine is poisoned?" the palace maid demanded severely.

"I dare not!" replied the crown prince.

"In that case, wouldn't you be an unfilial son by declining to drink the wine bestowed by His Majesty?"

The crown prince sat down reluctantly to the wine and dates. After drinking half of the pot, he pleaded, "I cannot drink anymore. Let me finish the rest of the wine on my return." However, the palace maid would not allow him to do so. After drinking the rest of the wine, the crown prince became bleary-eyed and muddle-headed.

Just then another palace maid came out and told him to copy a document. "What is this?" he asked sleepily. "A minister has composed a praper on your behalf for His Majesty's health and longevity, but you have to copy it yourself." The crown prince managed to scrawl down the article on the piece of silk he was given, though he had no inkling what it was about and made many mistakes and omissions. After that he was taken back to his residence, where he immediately sank into blissful sleep.

The following morning Emperor Huidi made an unusual appearance in the main hall to hold an audience. When the court officials had congratulated him on his recovery, the emperor suddenly threw a piece of white silk to the floor and said sharply, "That treacherous son should be put to death for writing such a letter!" The ministers stared at one another in dismay, not daring to make any comment.

Zhang Hua bent down and picked up the silk. In cramped, nearly illegible handwriting, the letter read, "Your Majesty should take his own life, otherwise I will enter the palace to dispatch him. Empress Jia should also take her own life,..." Zhang Hua broke into a cold sweat and handed the silk to other officials. "This is a misfortune for our country," he muttered at last. "During the course of history the deposal of a crown prince has often brought about big turmoils. I beg Your Majesty look further into the matter before reaching his decision."

Another minister agreed. "This letter looks really strange," he said. "It is not unlikely that someone has fabricated it to frame the crown prince. The authenticity of the handwriting must be determined before any action can be taken against him."

After some time, palace attendants brought over many writings in the crown prince's hand. The ministers scrutinized them without reaching any conclusion. Emperor Huidi was at a loss as to what to do.

Just then a stodgy, fierce-looking woman in a resplendent garment walked in. It was none other than Empress Jia. Coming up to Emperor Huidi, she said decisively, "Since some people have spoken in his favor, he can be absolved from the death penalty. But to forestall undesirable consequences, he must be deposed and reduced to the rank of a commoner!" The hall was deathly quiet. The emperor stared at her blankly and licked his lips. Finally he said, "The empress's suggestion is accepted!"

Thus the crown prince was deposed and put under house arrest. The incident roused intense suspicion among the people of the palace. Before long the truth of the matter became known. The letter copied by the drunken crown prince had been composed by a renowned scholar Pan Yue on the instructions of Jia Mi. He had also added the missing words by imitating the crown prince's handwriting. Popular discontent against Empress Jia thus made another court coup inevitable.

Gold-Dust Wine

The unjustified deposal of the crown prince intensified many courtiers' discontent with the empress. They began to work together to bring about her downfall.

Sima Ya and Xu Chao had both served as imperial guards in the Eastern Palace, the residence of the crown prince. In order to restore Sima Yu back to power, they decided to seek the support of a powerful minister. The person they had their eyes on was Sima Lun, the Prince of Zhao, who was in command of a strong band of troops.

As a garrison commander away from the capital, Sima Lun and his trusted follower Sun Xiu had exploited the local people to such an extent that they rose up in revolt. It took a long time to pacify the area. Called back to the court, he escaped punishment by ingratiating himself with Empress Jia. Subsequently he was promoted to be grand mentor to the crown prince and a general of the imperial forces.

One day Sima Ya called on Sun Xiu and said to him, "The empress is a jealous and heartless woman. She has added to her many misdeeds with the unjustified deposal of the crown prince. The lack of an imperial heir means serious instability for the empire. Many court officials have lost faith, and some are plotting a coup. The Prince of Zhao and you have close connections with the empress and knew about the plot to depose the crown prince beforehand. Once a crisis breaks out in the court, neither of you will escape retaliation. For your own safety, why not take preemptive action?"

As he listened to the ghastly scenario Sun Xiu felt a cold shiver running down his spine. "In your opinion, what action shall we take?"

"Depose the empress and reinstate the crown prince," replied Sima Ya unhesitatingly.

"All right," Sun Xiu said. "I'll advise the Prince of Zhao to rid our country of that scourge!"

Without delay Sun Xiu went to Sima Lun and recounted his conversation with Sima Ya. After hearing him out, Sima Lun admitted the soundness of the argument. It would be indeed perilous to keep his allegiance to the empress, who would soon be under attack from all sides. Then Sun Xiu hit upon another idea. "With the empress deposed, the crown prince would return to power. But he is too stubborn and self-willed to submit to our manipulation. We cannot expect him to trust us whole-heartedly just because of our restoring him to power. In the case of an emergency, he might want to get rid of us for his convenience. Why don't we induce the empress to murder the crown prince, then use this as the pretext to get rid of the empress? In this way we can kill two birds with one stone."

Sima Lun grinned broadly. With the crown prince dead and the empress deposed, he could go on to arrogate all powers to himself.

By Sun Xiu's instigation a rumor began to circulate in the palace about a conspiracy among some courtiers to depose the empress and rehabilitate the crown prince. At this point Sun Xiu went to see Jia Mi. "Are you aware of the coming disaster?" he asked.

"What do you mean?" Jia Mi asked in astonishment.

"You helped the empress to depose the crown prince," Sun Xiu said. "When the crown prince comes back to power, you will die without a burial place!"

Deeply frightened, Jia Mi asked Sun Xiu to explain the situation. After recounting the rumor, Sun Xiu said, "There is no time to lose. You should advise the empress to eliminate the crown prince at once. Only then can peace be maintained in the palace!"

In the meantime the rumor had reached the ears of Jia Nanfeng, and Jia Mi's report finally prompted her to take action against the crown prince.

Imprisoned in the city of Xuchang, Sima Yu was always on guard against possible assassins. Sun Lü, a eunuch sent by Jia Nanfeng to poison him, failed to get a chance to do so. He replaced the attendants there and had Sima Yu placed in a secluded courtyard in order to starve him to death. However, someone managed to smuggle food to the prince. Left with no alternative, Sun Lü decided to carry out the mission with his own hand. He went to see Sima Yu and tried to make him swallow some poisonous pills. Sima Yu refused and, saying he had to relieve himself, slipped out of the room. Picking up a stone pestle from a mortar, Sun Lü ran after the prince and dealt him a deadly blow on the back of the head. Then he pounded the pestle repeatedly on the prince until he was sure he had killed him.

Afterward, Jia Nanfeng declared that Sima Yu had committed suicide and ordered the crown prince to be buried in the manner befitting an imperial prince.

But Sun Xiu's arrangement, the real cause of Sima Yu's death, became widely known. Sima Lun, the Prince of Zhao, sent for Sima Tong, the Prince of Liang, and for Sima Jiong, the Prince of Qi, for a secret rendezvous at which they devised a scheme to overthrow the empress. Late one night Sima Lun summoned the officers of the imperial guard. Waving a piece of paper in his hand, he announced, "Empress Jia has committed a most hideous crime by framing and murdering the crown prince! I have received His Majesty's edict to eliminate this traitor, and you must obey my command without fail. Those who achieve merits will be rewarded, and anyone who dares to disobey will have his entire family wiped out!" The officers were dissatisfied with Empress Jia and her cohorts, so they felt thrilled by the order to bring her down. Little did they suspect that the imperial edict in Sima Lun's hand had been forged by Sun Xiu.

With the imperial guards at his command, Sima Lun entered the palace and forced Emperor Huidi to summon Jia Mi to the Eastern Hall. It was not until Jia Mi had walked through the gate that he sensed something was wrong. He turned abruptly and ran toward Empress Jia's residence, with the guards close at his heels. "Save me, Empress!" he shouted. A guard caught up with him and beheaded him on the spot.

Hearing Jia Mi's cry for help, Jia Nanfeng came out to take a look, only to find herself face to face with Sima Jiong. "What are you doing here?" she demanded sharply. "I've received an imperial edict to arrest you!" announced the Prince of Qi. "Nonsense!" Jia Nanfeng cried. "Every imperial edict goes out from here! Where did you get that edict?" Not bothering to argue with her, Sima Jiong had her tied up and brought to the Eastern Hall.

Escorted into the hall, Jia Nanfeng realized what had happened and called out to the emperor for help. But Emperor Huidi only stared at her blankly, too frightened to say anything. "Your Majesty!" Jia Nanfeng wailed. "Only with me by your side can you sit squarely on that throne! Without me as your empress, your days as emperor will be numbered!" Emperor Huidi's lips trembled but failed to produce a sound.

By enumerating Jia Nanfeng's crimes, including the murder of the crown prince, Sima Lun forced Emperor Huidi to reduce her to the rank of a commoner and throw her into prison. Five days later he sent someone to bring her an imperial edict ordering her to take her own life by drinking a cup of wine mixed with gold dust. With tears in her eyes, Jia

Nanfeng drained the cup and ended her life. All her followers were hunted down and executed.

Consequently the Western Jin Dynasty entered a tumultuous period, with fierce internecine strife among members of the ruling family and revolts by minority peoples. A few years later the dynasty collapsed.

LADY LOU MAKES ROOM
FOR AN ALIEN PRINCE

During the Northern and Southern Dynasties (420-589) China became a contention ground for various warlords. One of them, Gao Huan, grew steadily in strength until he took control of north China. In 550 his son, Gao Yang, set up the Northern Qi Dynasty.

During his arduous struggle to build up the strength of his forces, Gao Huan enjoyed the unswerving loyalty and generous support of his wife, Lady Lou.

Lady Lou had been born into a wealthy family with many house servants and numerous horses and cattle. Attracted by her beauty and talent, as well as the wealth of her family, many elegant young men in the area came to court her, but she turned them down without exception, for she was determined to marry a true hero instead of a rich, flighty young man. Her dream was fulfilled at last. She found a hero in distress, married him, and helped him become the ruler of north China.

It was during a walk on the city gate that she spotted Gao Huan, then a shabbily dressed garrison soldier in his early twenties. From his imposing appearance and bearing, she decided she had found herself the right man.

A little more observation convinced her that the young soldier would go far in the world. She sent a maid to inquire him in secret and found out that he was still unmarried. Then she made him a gift of a large sum of money and encouraged him to come to her family to propose marriage.

For Gao Huan, the self-surrender of such a beauty seemed too good to be true. Without delay he called on the Lou family, offering the money he had received from her as his

betrothal gift. Lady Lou did not turn her suitor down this time, and her parents were pleasantly surprised. Besides they thought, judging by his betrothal gift, the man must have come from a decent family. Thus they readily gave their consent.

After getting married, Lady Lou gave Gao Huan all the money she had so that he could build up a force of his own. One of Gao Huan's ancestors had been an official exiled to this city along with his family. By the time of his birth the family was living in utter destitution. Gao Huan grew up to be a handsome, generous young man and he joined the army, but remained an ordinary soldier because of his lack of means. Now that he had plenty of money at his disposal, he managed to enlist men under his service. Before long he was commanding a band of his own troops.

At that time China's north and south were under separate rulers. The north was divided among various military leaders, who were busily expanding their forces with a view to unifying the empire.

Uncomplainingly, Lady Lou did all she could to help her husband fulfill his ambition. She accompanied him from place to place, cooking his meals, mending his clothes, and sharing all his hardships. Deeply moved, Gao Huan resolved to live up to her expectations. With tremendous effort he established himself as the most powerful military leader in north China. Later, his second son, Gao Yang, proclaimed the founding of the Northern Qi Dynasty.

Over the years Gao Huan recognized his wife's unusual capabilities and often consulted her before taking a major decision. When he went on an expedition, Lady Lou took over control at their home base. Despite her family background she was content to live a plain life, with less than ten servants to wait upon her. Generous in nature and free of jealousy, she treated Gao Huan's consorts with kindness and solicitude. Therefore she gained universal respect.

On one occasion, when Gao Huan was out on an expedition, Lady Lou gave birth late at night to twins. During the gestation period she seemed to be in critical condition, and her attendants asked permission to inform Gao Huan at once. "He is leading the troops on an expedition," she said. "How can he leave his officers and men merely for my sake? After all, a person's fate is determined by heaven. Even if he could come back, what difference would it make?"

When Gao Huan learned about this, he treated Lady Lou with increased devotion and respect. She bore him two daughters and six sons, three of whom later became emperors.

Despite his devotion to Lady Lou, Gao Huan, like most rulers, could not help seeking pleasure from other women. Beautiful maidens made up part of the spoils from his victorious battles, and he did not hesitate to add them to his harem. Though Lady Lou raised no objection, the crowded harem inevitably became a hotbed of unrest.

Gao Huan was especially fond of a consort named Zheng because of her surpassing beauty. When he was away on expeditions, which was quite often, Lady Zheng had to stay behind like the other consorts. Unable to endure such lapse of attention, she began to eye Gao Huan's eldest son, a very handsome and elegant young man.

Back from his expedition, Gao Huan was informed of the affair by a house maid. Flying into a rage, he gave his son a hundred strokes of a cane, put him under house arrest, and prepared to deprive him of the title of heir apparent. He also had Lady Lou imprisoned, blaming her for failing to instruct her son properly and vowing never to see her again.

In distress the guilty son turned to Sima Ziru for help. Sima Ziru was a long-time follower of Gao Huan, and he felt sympathy for Lady Lou. So he went to Gao Huan and bombarded him with questions such as, "Who gave you the money to raise your own troops? Who nursed your wounds? Who chose to share hardships with you over a life of security and wealth? Who tended after you when you drifted from place to place? Now that you have attained fame and position, how can you forget this very person? How can you blame such a highly respected person on account of a trivial family matter?"

As if awakened from a dream, Gao Huan admitted his mistake at once and decided to make amends with his wife and son. A happy family reunion ensued.

The state of Rouran, which bordered on the northern frontier, suddenly lined up its powerful troops in preparation for an invasion. After consulting his advisors, Gao Huan decided to sue for peace by proposing intermarriage between the two ruling families. An envoy was dispatched to ask for the hand of the Rouran princess on behalf of Gao Huan's eldest son. The Rouran chieftain, however, replied that he would marry his daughter to none but Gao Huan himself. In other words, the Rouran troops would not withdraw unless Gao Huan divorced Lady Lou and married the Rouran princess.

Gao Huan faltered. He was in his fifties, with grown up children and a thirty-year marriage with his devoted wife, Lady Lou. How could he substitute her by an alien princess? But how else could he fend off the overpowering Rouran troops?

When informed of the dilemma, Lady Lou said to Gao Huan, "This is a matter of life and death for our nation. Hesitate no more!" As soon as the Rouran princess arrived, Lady Lou moved out of her residence to make room for her. Deeply moved, Gao Huan went to salute her in gratitude. Lady Lou looked at him calmly, "To prevent the Rouran princess from taking offense," she said, "and to maintain peace along the border, I suggest we say farewell to each other and never meet again."

LADY DUGU,
A VIRTUOUS YET
JEALOUS EMPRESS

At fourteen Lady Dugu married Yang Jian (reigned 581-604), or Emperor Wendi, the founder of the Sui Dynasty. For a long time the couple enjoyed marital bliss.

Born of a general's family, Lady Dugu showed no interest in needlework as a child but was a voracious reader of history. Because of her forthright disposition and practical ability, Yang Jian not only loved and respected her but was also a little afraid of her.

At that time fairs were opened on the border at which Turks from the north traded with people of Sui. Once a Turkish merchant offered a chest of pearls at the price of eight million coins. When an official offered to buy the pearls for the empress, she flatly refused. "Pearls are not what our country needs," she said. "If I had the money, I would rather award it to the officers and men who have rendered meritorious service." The incident won her the admiration of the emperor and the respect of the courtiers.

Every morning Lady Dugu accompanied the emperor to the gate of the main hall, where he would hold audience with his courtiers. Some of Lady Dugu's attendants were always present to observe the emperor's work, and they were instructed to speak up if he should make a mistake. When Yang Jian left the hall after the audience, Lady Dugu would accompany him back to their bedchamber to enjoy some less strenuous time together. Throughout Chinese history very few empresses could compare with Lady Dugu in her genuine concern for state affairs and strict and often beneficial supervision of the emperor's daily work.

Though orphaned at an early age, Lady Dugu put great stress on filial devotion. It was her habit to bestow presents on the parents of the courtiers. To the imperial princesses she admonished, "The princesses of the earlier dynasty were lacking in womanly virtues and showed disrespect toward their parents-in-law. Such a cold and indifferent attitude toward one's kith and kin is highly objectionable. You must guard against it."

Humane and kindhearted, Lady Dugu always shed tears of pity when the Court of Judicial Review carried out executions. When a half-brother of hers was found guilty of employing witchcraft to imprecate her and was sentenced to death according to law, she went on a three-day fast to persuade the emperor to spare the criminal. "If he were guilty of outrage against the people, I would not dare to say anything," she asserted. "Since he merely tried to harm me, I beseech Your Majesty to pardon him." Finally her half-brother was relieved of the death penalty.

On another occasion Lady Dugu's cousin committed a serious offense. When Yang Jian offered to spare him for her sake, she objected. "His crime was against the state," she said. "How can we put personal feelings before national interests?" Her cousin was subsequently beheaded.

For all her exemplary virtues Lady Dugu was excessively jealous. An ardent believer in the principle of monogamy, she hardly ever allowed the emperor to spend the night with his consorts, who could only lament their hapless fate.

As the years went by the empress gradually lost her beauty and luster, and the emperor became more and more attracted to the younger, fresher women in his harem. A frail beauty named Weichi caught his attention, and he often sought her company in secret. Lady Dugu, however, found out about the affair and vented her anger on the poor maiden.

While the emperor was holding audience one day, Lady

Dugu had Weichi killed and sent someone to bring a box to the emperor at the end of the audience. When the box was opened, the emperor stared aghast. It contained the head of his favorite, still dripping with blood.

Speechless with fury, Yang Jian leapt onto a horse and galloped out of the palace. Some courtiers ran after him and finally caught up with him in a mountain valley. When they begged him to return, Yang Jian sighed deeply. "Though I am the emperor, I have no liberty!" The courtiers pleaded, "How can Your Majesty abandon the all under heaven because of a mere woman? Please return with us!" Yang Jian lingered in the valley for a long time. It was midnight when he finally returned to the palace.

Lady Dugu, who had been waiting anxiously, fell on her knees to beg his pardon. With the courtiers saying a few placating words, the emperor sent for food and wine and made peace with his empress. After that, Lady Dugu had no more outbursts of jealousy.

Lady Dugu's death at fifty at last left the emperor free for his carnal pursuits. Overreaching himself, he fell seriously ill and did not recover. On his deathbed he lamented to the attendants, "I would not have come to this if the empress were still alive!" But his repentance came too late, and he died soon afterwards.

EMPRESS ZHANGSUN ADMONISHES HER IMPERIAL HUSBAND

A contingent of chariots rode along the road leading to the Tang capital, Chang'an. In the first chariot sat Empress Zhangsun. Though over thirty, she had a slim figure, and her lovely face shone brightly with a smile. In her hand was a mulberry leaf.

Now and then she lifted the curtain to gaze out of the window. After an early morning drizzle, the trees, grass and grain seedlings looked greener than usual, and there was a fresh fragrance in the air. She could hear chickens crowing and dogs barking from the villages in the distance, and see kitchen smoke rising from the farmhouses.

Under its second ruler, Li Shimin, or Emperor Taizong (reigned 626-649), the Tang empire underwent a period of rehabilitation. To enable the people to recover from war damages, Li Shimin proclaimed tax reductions and refrained from using conscript labor for construction of imperial palaces and gardens. Labor conscription was restricted to the building of defense works during the slack season. Policies implemented to promote agricultural production won widespread support from the people.

Gazing into the distance Empress Zhangsun murmured, "At last the people have settled down to a peaceful life after so many years of tumult."

She had just finished a trip with the imperial consorts to plant mulberry trees and grow silkworms, a gesture by the court to accentuate the importance of farming and silk culture. Conscious of the difficulties facing the country, she resolved

to help her husband as much as she could. She hoped to set an example for the people by her diligence and thrift, qualities in great need for rebuilding the empire.

She was reminded of a recent incident. The wet nurse of the crown prince had come to her and complained that the crown prince didn't have enough material possessions for daily use, to which she retorted, "What I am really concerned about is whether the crown prince can cultivate his virtue properly and gain universal fame and respect, and you have the duty to lead him onto the right path. Stop worrying over his lack of material possessions!" The wet nurse had retired shame-facedly.

Memory of this incident brought a sigh to Lady Zhangsun's lips. "It is no easy thing to establish an empire," she muttered, "but to govern it is even more difficult!"

The chariots arrived at the palace. Empress Zhangsun had just enough time to wash and make up when Emperor Taizong came. "In your tree-planting trip, you must have seen the local scenery," he remarked.

"I have seen the people living in peace and contentment," she replied. "Such a situation is hard won, and I hope Your Majesty will cherish it."

"Indeed I will!" Emperor Taizong responded. "You always have the welfare of the state at heart and you keep giving me good advice. Heaven must have sent you to assist me!" Then he said, "By the way, there is something I want to tell you. Your elder brother, Zhangsun Wuji, has followed me through thick and thin all these years. I intend to give him a promotion."

Empress Zhangsun was surprised. It had been her long-time policy to refrain from participating in proceedings involving the imperial court. Whenever Emperor Taizong consulted her on such matters, she would decline to make comment, saying, "Being a woman, I can only attend to my household duties in the rear palace. Affairs of the court are beyond my scope." Emperor Taizong was much impressed by her self-restraint.

However, this time it was different, and she felt compelled to speak her mind. "Thanks to the imperial favor bestowed on me, my family has enjoyed unsurpassed honor and prestige. I really don't think it suitable for my brother to be made a high official. Abuse of power by external relatives can be calamitous for the nation."

Well read in history, Li Shimin was fully aware that external relatives had often created trouble by abusing their power and even attempting to usurp the throne. However, he had complete trust in Zhangsun Wuji and was going to promote him solely because of his ability, not because of his kinship with the imperial family. "I know what you have in mind," he said to the empress. "Your brother will be chosen on the basis of his merits. I will not use a man without talent even if he is a close relative, and I will be ready to use a truly talented man even if he was my enemy."

Failing to dissuade the emperor, Lady Zhangsun sent for her elder brother and explained the situation to him. "I don't think it a good idea for another Zhangsun to become a high official," she said. "That would sow the seeds of trouble." Zhangsun Wuji readily agreed.

The next day, when Emperor Taizong offered the promotion to Zhangsun Wuji, he declined most determinedly. The emperor was thus compelled to give up the idea.

Empress Zhangsun had a daughter who received the title Princess of Changle. When she was going to get married, the entire palace was bustling in preparation for her wedding. To show his consideration for the empress, Li Shimin decided to give her daughter twice as much of a dowry as he had his own elder sister, titled the Elder Princess. When a minister named Wei Zheng learned of this, he tried to discourage the emperor by citing an historical example. "When Emperor Mingdi of Han elevated his son, he remarked, 'How can my son compare with those of the late emperor?' Therefore the land area given of his son had only half the size and population of that given to any of the late emperor's sons. Now Your Majesty wants to give your own daughter twice as much of a dowry as that given to the Elder Princess, who is the daughter of the late emperor. Is this appropriate in the light of what Emperor Mingdi of Han did?"

Li Shimin felt affronted, but he did not show it. Instead, he pretended to be glad to adopt the advice. "Wei Zheng's words are reasonable," he announced to the other ministers. "The dowry of the Princess of Changle will be half as much as that of the Elder Princess."

Lady Zhangsun noticed his sullen mood when he returned from the audience. "Did anything unpleasant take place to-day?" she inquired. After he described the incident to her, she was delighted, saying, "I heard you praise Wei Zheng many times but did not know why. Today he spoke up to correct your mistake in the name of propriety, asking you to place rules and rites before personal interests. He is truly a pillar of the state! Though I am your wife, I often take my cue from you in my speech and conduct for fear of offending you. Wei Zheng is merely a subject of yours, and yet he does not hesitate to point out your mistake whenever it is necessary. You must not ignore his advice!"

Li Shimin was much mollified by her words.

A few days later Li Shimin returned from the audience, looking angry. "Someday I will put Wei Zheng to death!" he blurted out to Lady Zhangsun. Dismayed, she asked him to explain the reason. "Humph!" Li Shimin grunted, breathing heavily. "How dare he insult me in front of my courtiers? What impudence! Maybe he assumes I can do nothing about him. Well, I am the Son of Heaven! If I want somebody dead, he can't stay alive!"

Lady Zhangsun realized that once more Wei Zheng had offended the emperor by his blunt criticism. As Li Shimin sat there fuming, she retired to her bedchamber, from which she emerged a moment later in her court dress. She bowed to the emperor, who gave a start. "Why are you wearing this dress?" he asked. "You know it is only for special occasions such as when you receive a title, attend a sacrifice or a court meeting."

Straight-faced, Lady Zhangsun replied, "According to what I have heard, only a sage ruler can have honest, outspoken subjects. If Wei Zheng can repeatedly offer his advice without reserve, it is only because of your sagacity. Allow me to offer my congratulations!"

Li Shimin's rage was turned into joy. "Thank you for pointing this out to me," he said. "I nearly made a serious mistake. Tomorrow morning I will apologize to Wei Zheng to relieve him of any doubts."

"It will be a blessing for the great Tang empire if Your Majesty can accept criticism with such grace and trust loyal and honest men," she said.

After that, Lady Zhangsun had a handsome present given to Wei Zheng along with her message: "I hope Wei Zheng will remain honest and outspoken till the end!" Moved, Wei Zheng pledged, "I will do my best for the great Tang!"

In an unusually sultry summer Lady Zhangsun fell ill. It was a relapse of the asthma that she had contracted at an early age. When the imperial physician failed to relieve her condition, the crown prince suggested, "Mother, let me ask His Majesty to proclaim a general amnesty. Maybe the gods will be moved to relent a little and allow you to recover from this illness."

Lady Zhangsun opened her eyes, looking very grave. After a pause for breath, she said to the crown prince, "You must not do that! If the gods will reward a person for his good deeds, I deserve such a reward because I have stayed away from evil all my life. If I had done evil, it would be too late to try to move the gods by an amnesty. Moreover, amnesty is a matter of great importance to the state, therefore it should not be proclaimed merely for my sake. I would fain die right away than have you meet the emperor with such a suggestion!"

The crown prince did not bring up the matter with the emperor, but went to seek help from Chief Minister Fang Xuanling, who presented a memorial to Li Shimin. Li Shimin would have acted on this advice and declared a national amnesty had it not been for Lady Zhangsun's adamant objection.

At this juncture Fang Xuanling committed a minor mistake in his office. Li Shimin, who was in a gloomy mood because of Lady Zhangsun's lingering illness, flew into a rage and deprived Fang of his post.

Lady Zhangsun's condition continued to deteriorate. At last she bade farewell to her husband. "Chief Minister Fang Xuanling has served you for a long time and has carried out his duties conscientiously. A minor mistake does not justify his dismissal from office. My family members have been bathed in imperial favor all these years and have done little to deserve this. I beseech my lord never to grant a high position or noble title to any of them. One more thing. I have no use for an elaborate funeral or ornate grave. Just have me buried at the foot of a hill. Please grant me these little requests!"

Her words were interrupted by a fit of violent coughing. After regaining her breath, she took Li Shimin by the hand and went on. "I hope Your Majesty will bestow favor on men of virtue and keep petty sycophants at a distance, accept just criticism and ignore slanderous talk, cut down on taxes and labor conscription to relieve the people's burden, and refrain from overindulgence in pleasure trips and merry-making. I will have no cause for worry if Your Majesty promises to act in this way!"

Li Shimin was choked with emotion. Restraining his grief, he forced a smile and nodded his assent. Lady Zhangsun closed her eyes for the last time. In that year she was only thirty-six.

For a long time afterward Li Shimin sat alone all day, lost in the memory of his dear empress. He remembered the many adversities she had gone through with him when he was fighting rival warlords for control of the empire. With him on the throne, she concerned herself with affairs of the state in addition to fulfilling her duties in the rear palace. Her timely advice had steered him away from many a pitfall. But now she was gone forever, unable to utter another word to him. As he ran these thoughts in his mind, Li Shimin was overcome with grief and felt the urge to burst out crying.

A few days after Lady Zhangsun's death, Li Shimin gratified her wish by reinstating Fang Xuanling as Chief Minister.

EMPRESS WU ZETIAN

During Li Shimin's reign, one of his courtiers had a lovely daughter whose visage induced a experienced necromancer to predict that she would one day become ruler of all under heaven. That girl was named Wu Zetian.

In the meantime, a secret book circulating among the people carried these words: "After three Tang emperors, Empress Wu will rule all under heaven." When a courtier got hold of a copy he hastened to report it to Li Shimin, who was greatly startled by the news. A necromancer, when he was four, had predicted after examining his visage, "He has the posture of a dragon and phoenix. At twenty he will bring peace and prosperity to the world!" And the prediction came true. Therefore the rumor about an empress Wu taking over control of the empire from the Li family made him quite nervous.

Three Things to Tame a Horse

At fourteen Wu Zetian was so renowned for her beauty that the emperor decided to take her into the palace. Her mother felt very sad, not knowing what her future would be. Wu Zetian, however, was calm and assured. "Why should you be so sorrowful?" she said to her mother. "How do you know it won't turn out to be good fortune for us?"

In the imperial harem a beautiful woman like Wu Zetian was not hard to find. At first she failed to attract the emperor's attention and lived as an ordinary palace maid. As the years rolled on, she even began to doubt if she would ever emerge from obscurity.

Li Shimin had a horse that was so bad-tempered that no one could tame it. One day he examined the horse in the company of his consorts, who all agreed that it was a fine

horse. However, no one dared walk close to it. Li Shimin grumbled to himself, "Is there no one to tame it?" As soon as he said this, a palace maid stepped forward. "Your Majesty, I can tame it!"

Li Shimin looked at Wu Zetian in surprise. "Really? How can a frail woman like you deal with such a ferocious animal?"

"By using three things," replied Wu Zetian.

"What are these things?" Li Shimin asked, his interest aroused.

"I need a whip, a flog, and a dagger. First I will whip the horse, then I will beat its head with the flog. If this still fails to tame it, I will cut its throat with the dagger!"

All the consorts present gasped in awe. Wu Zetian thus succeeded in raising herself in the emperor's estimation and gaining a reputation in the palace.

However, as a battle-seasoned commander as well as sage ruler, Li Shimin had no taste for brave and forthright women. He preferred his consorts to be graceful, frail beauties. Therefore Wu Zetian failed to win his favor. On the other hand the crown prince, Li Zhi, a sickly, timid young man, was fascinated by the unusual bravery displayed by this comely lady, who was four years his senior. A clandestine attachment developed between them.

When Li Shimin died of illness, Li Zhi ascended the throne at twenty-two. As dictated by palace rules, upon the ascension of the new emperor, the late emperor's consorts who had not borne any children would be discharged from the palace. Some of them were assigned to be nuns at Ganye Monastery. Dressed in black, they left the palace in a downcast mood, lamenting not so much the decease of their imperial master as their own hapless fate. Among these was Wu Zetian. At twenty-six, she felt as if her life had come to a dead end, and the new emperor seemed to have forgotten her altogether.

Death of the Little Princess

For Wu Zetian, the days spent in the monastery were agonizingly long. A year later, on the anniversary of Li Shimin's death, Li Zhi paid a visit to Ganye Monastery, where he saw Wu Zetian again. News of their tearful meeting spread quickly in the capital. Informed of the incident, Empress Wang felt bitter yet glad. She had been worrying over the emperor's partiality toward his consort Lady Xiao, so she planned to employ Wu Zetian to counter the influence of this hateful rival. She would get great benefit from this arrangement, and both the emperor and Wu Zetian would also be pleased.

Shortly after the meeting at the monastery, Empress Wang had Wu Zetian taken into the palace in secret. Overjoyed, Li Zhi spent that very night in her company. She became the emperor's favorite, much to the distress of the now neglected Lady Xiao.

At first Wu Zetian showed her gratitude to Empress Wang by her modest and respectful attitude. The unsuspecting empress often spoke in her favor to Li Zhi. A few years later Wu Zetian, having given birth to two sons, was elevated to the position next to the empress. Only then did Empress Wang realize that her plan to diminish Lady Xiao's influence with Wu Zetian was only too successful. She now had to form an alliance with Lady Xiao to fight Wu Zetian, their common enemy.

However, the two women proved no match for Wu Zetian, who had not experienced the ups and downs in the palace without growing quite sophisticated. She enlisted many palace attendants into her service. As Li Shimin was partial toward women with poetic and literary talents, she found she had to read extensively, gaining a good knowledge of history. Compared with her, both Empress Wang and Lady Xiao were simple, artless women.

As she had lifted Wu Zetian from obscurity, Empress Wang expected gratitude and humility in return. Wu Zetian, however, had other, more practical considerations. She was fully aware that the imperial harem was a place of constant strife, intrigue, and hidden crisis. The only way to attain an impregnable position was to become empress herself and to have her son elevated as the crown prince. With his generous disposition and lack of judgement, the emperor was subject to others' influence or even manipulation. Wu Zetian decided to employ her wiles against her benefactor, the empress.

While sparing no effort to ingratiate herself with the emperor, Wu Zetian enlisted many informers in the palace to keep a wary eye on Empress Wang and Lady Xiao. Whenever she heard something to their disadvantage, she went at once to inform the emperor. Li Zhi thus began to regard his empress with increasing disapproval.

Soon after, Wu Zetian gave birth to a baby girl. Chubby and creamy-skinned, the little princess became a favorite of the emperor. One day at noon Wu Zetian was sitting by her sleeping child when a maid reported that the empress was coming to visit her. Wu Zetian thought for a moment, sent all the attendants away, and then left the room herself. "How is the little princess?" Empress Wang asked when she came to the door, but there was no one to answer her. Entering the room, she found herself alone with the baby. She sat down and watched it for a while and, when Wu Zetian failed to show up, left the room.

Late in the day Li Zhi returned from the audience looking high-spirited. "Where is the little princess?" he asked Wu Zetian when she came out to meet him. "I miss her a lot after a day's separation."

Wu Zetian took the baby from the cradle. "Everyone loves the little princess!" she said, smiling brightly. All of a sudden, her voice turned shrill. "Your Majesty! Look at her!"

Li Zhi gave a start. The little princess looked ashen, her

body felt cold, and she was not breathing anymore. "How did this happen?" Li Zhi roared thunderously. "How did you look after the little princess?"

Wu Zetian threw herself on the ground and broke into tears. "When the little princess was asleep at noon, I was invited by Lady Xiao to go to her place, and I returned only a moment ago. It was all my fault!" She began to wail uncontrollably.

Li Zhi turned to the attending maids. "Confess! Who murdered the little princess?" Cowering in fear, they all pleaded innocence.

"Was there any visitor?" Li Zhi demanded.

"Yes, Your Majesty," a maid replied. "Empress Wang came."

"Was there anyone else in the room with her?" Wu Zetian asked hastily.

"No. She stayed for a little while, then left."

"What does this mean?" Wu Zetian cried. "Could the empress have...." Before she could finish the sentence, she passed out.

"I will depose the empress at once!" Li Zhi bellowed.

When Li Zhi announced his intention of deposing of Empress Wang and replacing her with Wu Zetian, most of his courtiers objected by saying that Empress Wang had done nothing to deserve such a treatment. Furthermore, they thought Wu Zetian unfit to be the empress because she had been a consort of the late emperor. Much to Wu Zetian's exasperation, the emperor faltered in the face of such vigorous opposition.

During the heated argument at court one old minister kept silent. The emperor noticed this and urged him to express his opinion. "Whoever you choose for your empress is a family matter," came the reply. "Why is there any need to ask the opinion of outsiders?" Li Zhi, pleasantly surprised, immediately issued an edict reducing both Empress Wang and Lady Xiao to the rank of commoners and setting Wu Zetian up as the new empress and her eldest son the crown prince. At last Wu Zetian got what she had been dreaming for. But that did not stop her from wanting more.

No Cats Allowed in the Palace

The disgraced Lady Wang and Lady Xiao were locked up in a secluded corner of the palace. The house was surrounded by high walls; there was no window, just a small opening in the gate through which meals were passed to them three times a day. The place was heavily guarded. As if plunged into an abyss, they were filled with despair and grief over their misfortune.

One day it suddenly occurred to Li Zhi to pay them a visit. Arriving at the place, he found the gate locked and peered into the small opening, but it was too dark to see anything. A surge of pity and remorse filled the emperor's heart. "Where are you, my Empress and Lady of Excellence?"

Hearing the emperor's voice at the gate, Lady Wang and Lady Xiao burst into tears, almost too agitated to speak. "If Your Majesty for old time's sake is kind enough to let us see the sky again, please rename this place 'Courtyard of Forgiveness'."

With tears in his eyes, Li Zhi replied, "I will have it done promptly."

Wu Zetian was soon informed of the incident. She immediately had the two ladies beaten black and blue with cudgels. Still unappeased, she had their limbs cut off, then had them thrown into big wine jars. A few days later both ladies died of the torture. Before her death, Lady Xiao cursed Wu Zetian bitterly, saying, "I will change into a cat in my next life, and may you change into a mouse! I will bite through your throat to avenge myself!"

Unable to get Lady Xiao's curse off her mind, Wu Zetian trembled with fear whenever she heard a cat meowing. Therefore she forbade the palace women to keep cats. Even so she had frequent nightmares in which she was brought face to face with Lady Wang and Lady Xiao, their hair disheveled and their bodies soaked in blood. Thus she decided to move out of Chang'an and live in the eastern capital, Luoyang.

Forestalling a Court Coup

The emperor, Li Zhi, suffered from migraine headaches that made his reading of memorials and documents an ordeal. Therefore he often delegated his regal duties to his empress, who fully relished her chance to wield power at the imperial court.

As the emperor's authority was being increasingly arrogated by Wu Zetian, some quick-minded officials began to curry favor with her, and she took the chance to enlist her own followers and to suppress her opponents. By her arrangement one old minister who had adamantly opposed her elevation to empress was demoted, exiled, and finally forced to commit suicide.

Quite a few courtiers loyal to the imperial family were outraged by Wu Zetian's unscrupulous behavior and plotted to have her deposed. In the meantime the emperor also began to feel dissatisfied with her overbearing manners. On several occasions he found himself unable to carry things through because of her obstruction. As a result, he was not averse to the idea of deposing her. A courtier named Shangguan Yi, who had spoken most vehemently against Wu Zetian's arrogation of imperial power, was assigned to compose the edict to depose the empress.

At a critical moment one of the emperor's attending maids informed Wu Zetian of the news. Hastening to the hall, Wu Zetian demanded to know what she had done to deserve such a betrayal. Not daring to tell her the true reason, Li Zhi groped for excuses but found none. Weeping bitterly, Wu Zetian pleaded, argued and remonstrated with the emperor until he broke down and blurted out, "It is Shangguan Yi who talked me into this!"

Leaving the emperor, Wu Zetian worked with her followers to bring a trumped-up charge against Shangguan Yi, who was subsequently executed.

Supreme Ruler of the Empire

After the aborted coup against her, Wu Zetian began to preside over the court together with Li Zhi. While he discussed state affair with his courtiers, she listened from behind a curtain and had the final say on all issues, big or small. Thus she became the de facto ruler of the empire, with Li Zhi reduced to a puppet. He was emperor for thirty-four years, but the last twenty years of his reign was merely nominal. Wu Zetian's authority in the imperial court became supreme.

The crown prince, named Li Hong, was Wu Zetian's eldest son. He gained wide respect among the courtiers when the emperor, during a spell of illness, appointed him to hold court on the emperor's behalf. But Wu Zetian would not allow anyone, not even her own son, to stand in the way of her ambitions. Moreover, Li Hong often spoke up against her excesses. She began to bear an intense dislike for him.

As Li Zhi's health worsened, it seemed that the crown prince did not have to wait long to succeed to the throne. When that day came, Wu Zetian would be compelled to surrender her control of the court and return to the rear palace. For her, that prospect looked more ghastly than death. Shortly thereafter, the crown prince mysteriously died of food poisoning in the palace.

Wu Zetian made her second son the new crown prince, but he soon fell out of her favor and was reduced to the rank of a commoner. Thereupon she made her third son the crown prince. This son finally ascended the throne when Li Zhi died of illness. Soon after, he was deposed by Wu Zetian, who put her fourth son on the throne. As the empress dowager, Wu

Zetian continued to preside over the court. Her fourth son lived in constant trepidation, not knowing what was in store for him. Finally he decided to call it a day and proposed to abdicate in favor of his mother. Wu Zetian was eager to comply. In the ninth month of 690, she ascended the throne and changed the dynastic name from Tang to Zhou. She was the first and only empress in China to rule in her own capacity.

During the fifty years that she presided over the court, Wu Zetian, though lacking in benevolence, proved herself a diligent and capable ruler. She introduced political and social reforms with remarkable results.

In early seventh century the disparity of wealth became very acute in the rural areas. The landowners who had accumulated considerable wealth began to demand a higher social status. In order to gain their support, Wu Zetian took measures to satisfy their needs. Traditionally, social hierarchy was established on the basis of noble titles and official ranks restricted to the few privileged families or clans, which were listed in an official book of family names. Whatever his merits, a man bearing an ordinary family name had little chance of upgrading his social status. At Wu Zetian's order, the book of prestigious names was revised to include those obtaining official posts by rendering meritorious service. Thus a soldier who fought bravely on the frontier could aspire to not only promotion but glorification of his family name. The gap between aristocracy and common folks was reduced drastically.

During Wu Zetian's reign the system of civil recruitment examinations was expanded and perfected, with more successful candidates selected each year than ever before. In this way talented men had a better chance of advancing themselves and obtaining official posts. People with humble origins began to serve as officials in the imperial court, which had hitherto been dominated by a few powerful clans. Wu Zetian also appointed many scholars as advisors with the responsibility of discussing state affairs and handling memorials. Most of them came from the class of wealthy landowners.

Wu Zetian's reforms met with opposition from some of the powerful clans and high officials, who staged an aborted coup to depose her and restore the reign of the Li family.

By employing brutal torture and offering high rewards to informants, Wu Zetian embarked on a merciless campaign of suppressing her political opponents until no one dared challenge her authority. In the meantime she tried to enlist capable people to her service by encouraging self-recommendation by any official or even commoner. In many instances she bypassed convention to recruit men of talent. On the other hand, whenever she found any official to be incompetent, she did not hesitate to have him dismissed or even executed.

During Wu Zetian's reign there was a marked growth in population, from less than four million households in 652 preceding her dominance of the court, to over six million in 705, the year of her abdication.

Peace and prosperity, however, gave rise to rampant corruption among the members of the ruling class. The oversized bureaucracy ate up huge chunks of the state revenue. Large scale construction of palace buildings further depleted national resources. On one occasion, when copper and iron was in short supply, Wu Zetian ordered an amassment of farm tools to meet the need. A believer in Buddha, she spent a huge amount of money and manpower on building Buddhist temples all across the empire.

Border conflicts began to escalate, and sometimes turned into invasions causing great misery of the common people. The nation's inland suffered natural calamities from floods and droughts, with the inevitable result of widespread famine; over half of the population in the stricken area either starved to death or became vagrant beggars. But this did not stop the imperial court from employing conscript labor on a large scale. Driven to despair, some peasants rose in revolt.

Internal strife within the imperial court also intensified. Some officials were waiting anxiously for a chance to depose Wu Zetian and restore the empire to the rule of the Li family.

Advanced in years, Wu Zetian found herself caught between reminiscence of her arduous journey to the throne and forebodings about the future. The time had come to designate the heir apparent, but she could not make up her mind whether to choose her nephew or her son. After all, her nephew bore the family name of Wu. She finally consulted a powerful courtier, who answered, "Which tie is stronger—that between mother and son or aunt and nephew? Give it a little thought, and Your Majesty will reach her decision!" Acting on this advice, Wu Zetian recalled her third son, Li Xian, back to the palace and erected him as the crown prince.

At eighty-one Wu Zetian grew too ill to move out of her bed. Courtiers loyal to the Li family rose up against her, demanding that she abdicate in favor of the crown prince. With great reluctance, Wu Zetian agreed. Thereupon Li Xian ascended the throne and restored the dynastic title to Tang.

In the eleventh month of 705 Wu Zetian died of illness and anguish. She was buried in the same grave as the late Emperor Gaozong. By her will, her gravestone carried no epitaph, signifying her conviction that posterity would give a just appraisal of her merits and demerits.

THE PLUM CONSORT

The Plum Consort, named Jiang Caiping, was discovered by Gao Lishi, head eunuch of Emperor Xuanzong (reigned 711-755), and brought into the palace to wait upon the emperor.

A typical beauty from south China, Jiang was a book lover and could write elegant poetry and prose. Despite her talents she had a quiet disposition and preferred to wear simple clothes and light make-up.

Her residence was surrounded by her favorite flower, the plum blossom. A placard hanging above the gate carried the inscription "Plum Pavilion" in Emperor Xuanzong's own handwriting. When the plum blossoms were in full bloom, Jiang would linger there all day, sometimes late into the night, feasting her eyes on their rare beauty and composing poems to convey her sentiment. Because of this the emperor nick-named her "the Plum Consort."

Soon after her entry into the palace Jiang won Emperor Xuanzong's exclusive favor. The other consorts, who often fought among themselves for the emperor's attention, knew better than to compete with her. Apart from her literary talents, Jiang also played several musical instruments and had superb dancing and singing skills. Once, Emperor Xuanzong was playing a competitive game with her while the imperial princes looked on. After losing repeatedly to her, Emperor Xuanzong smiled and remarked to the princes, "She must be a plum fairy! Last time, when I gave her a white jade flute, she enchanted all of us with her beautiful song and dance. And today she has beat me time and again in this game."

"This is a mere game," Jiang hastily replied, "and I have won by chance. The true worth of Your Majesty lies in securing peace and prosperity for the entire nation and bestowing benefits on all your subjects. How unworthy am I in comparison!"

Emperor Xuanzong, immensely pleased, praised Jiang for her insight and sagacity.

For quite a long time Emperor Xuanzong was enthralled by the graceful manners and simple charms of his Plum Consort. Then all of a sudden, Yang Yuhuan, one of the most renowned beauties in Chinese history, entered upon the scene. Plump, voluptuous and bewitching, she took the emperor's breath away and soon usurped the position of the Plum Consort.

The Plum Consort and Lady Yang, entitled the Honored Consort, got along like fire and water. Each had her unique style and charms, so that the emperor did not want to have to choose between them. He liked to compare himself to Shun, the ancient sage king whose two wives, Ehuang and Nüying, got along wonderfully. However, Lady Yang had little tolerance for her rival. As the emperor became more and more enamored of her, he was compelled to give up the Plum Consort by sending her away to the eastern palace.

But memories of their happy days together still lingered in the emperor's mind. One night, when Lady Yang happened to be away, Emperor Xuanzong sent a trusted attendant to escort Jiang to his residence. Afraid of being discovered, the attendant dared not light a lantern or utter any sound. The reunion plunged the Plum Consort into tears of joy intermingled with sorrow.

At daybreak the attendant hurried in. "The Honored Consort has come!"

Emperor Xuanzong got up in a fluster. He barely had time to hide his lover behind the curtain when Lady Yang stormed into the room, demanding a confession. He boldly denied having had the other women in his chambers, and the Honored Consort left in a fluff. When the emperor recovered a little from the shock, he told his Plum Consort to come out of hiding, only to find that she had been transported back to the eastern palace by the attendant. He vent his fury on the attendant and had him decapitated.

Emperor Xuanzong picked up Jiang's shoes and headwear and had them taken back to her. The Plum Consort burst into tears on receiving them, saying, "Does His Majesty really want to desert me?"

The envoy tried to soothe her. "His Majesty is not going to desert you. He just doesn't want to offend the Honored Consort."

Jiang broke into a bitter smile. "If His Majesty is afraid of offending the Fat Consort for my sake, doesn't that mean he has deserted me?"

Jiang racked her brains trying to find a way to win back the emperor's favor. She remembered the story of Ahjiao, empress of Emperor Wudi of the Han Dynasty. In order to remind the emperor of the wonderful times he had shared with her, Ahjiao hired Sima Xiangru to write about her longings in a piece of beautiful prose. Though the plan fell short of success, Emperor Wudi had been moved upon reading the prose. Why couldn't she do the same? Maybe the emperor could be persuaded to return to her side.

The man Jiang approached about this matter was Gao Lishi, the emperor's most trusted eunuch. She offered him a thousand taels of silver if he would find her a talented scholar for the job. Gao, preoccupied with fawning on the Honored Consort, declined the offer, saying no contemporary scholar could come up with anything comparable to Sima Xiangru's masterpiece. Jiang then realized she was totally alone, with no one to rely on but herself. Thus she composed "Sorrow in the Eastern Tower" herself.

While Emperor Xuanzong was reading the Plum Consort's article, Lady Yang found out about it and roared angrily, "How dare that perverted slut vent her spleen like this? I hope

Your Majesty will grant her permission to hang herself!"

Emperor Xuanzong remained silent, lost in reminiscences of the many joys the Plum Consort had afforded him. In his mind's eye he envisaged her pining away in the eastern palace, her face sallow, her eyes filled with anguish. Her beloved plum trees, without her loving care, were probably withering away along with her.

After sending out her work, the Plum Consort often leaned against the door waiting for the emperor's sudden appearance. One day, at the sight of a mounted horseman, she asked her attendants, "Could this be His Majesty's envoy coming to fetch me?"

"The horseman comes from the south," one of the attendants replied. "He is a special envoy bringing fresh lichi to the Honored Consort!"

Her heart sinking, the Plum Consort burst into tears.

Feeling a little remorse yet unwilling to displease Lady Yang, Emperor Xuanzong finally sent an envoy to see the Plum Consort, making her the present of a chest of pearls.

When she received the pearls, the Plum Consort realized this was the emperor's lame answer to her appeal. She wrote a poem on the spot and gave it to the envoy to take back.

The poem, along with the chest of pearls, was brought to Emperor Xuanzong. The poem read:

> For days my eyebrows are unpainted,
> And my handkerchief soaked in tears.
> Since Your Majesty cares nothing for me,
> Why should I care for my looks?
> How can a mere chest of pearls
> Bring solace to my lonely existence?

The emperor was overcome with a sense of loss on reading the poem. He had it put to music and called the song "A Chest of Pearls" in honor of his Plum Consort.

Though only a short distance apart, the emperor and his

Plum Consort never met again. While the former indulged in various forms of merry-making in the company of his Honored Consort, Lady Yang, the latter pined away in total neglect and oblivion.

Then a revolt staged by a powerful general named An Lushan forced Emperor Xuanzong into exile. On his return to the capital, he had the palace thoroughly searched but could not find the Plum Consort. A handsome reward was offered for any clue as to her whereabouts. However, no one came to claim the reward. The emperor then sent for a renowned magician and charged him to seek information from the higher realm, but all these efforts were in vain.

To console the grieved emperor, a palace attendant brought him a portrait of the Plum Consort. But the portrait intensified the emperor's longing for her person. Perhaps moved by this singular devotion, she finally emerged in his dream. Covering her face by her sleeves, she said sobbingly, "When Your Majesty was away from the capital, I fell into the hands of the enemy troops and defended my chastity by death. I was buried under a plum tree by the pond."

Emperor Xuanzong woke up with a start and immediately sent men to dig by the Taiye Pond. When nothing was uncovered, he began to doubt the authenticity of his dream. It suddenly occurred to him that the Taiye Pond, where the Honored Consort had taken frequent baths, was an unlikely burial place for the Plum Consort. He led the attendants to a plum tree beside the hot spring pond, where they finally unearthed the body of the Plum Consort. A sword cut ran across the right side of her chest.

Emperor Xuanzong's grief was too deep for tears.

HONORED CONSORT
LADY YANG

At dawn, when the Shangyang Palace with all its trees and flowers was wrapped in the morning mist, the quiet spell was suddenly broken by a bitter quarrel.

"Where is that plum demon?" demanded Lady Yang, the Honored Consort.

"Isn't she in the eastern palace?" Emperor Xuanzong replied as he slipped out of bed.

"Really?" Lady Yang sniggered. "All right, I beseech Your Majesty to have her brought here at once. The two of us can enjoy a warm bath together!"

At this time the Plum Consort had fallen out of favor with the emperor and had been sent to live in a secluded corner of the palace. But the emperor had not forgotten her completely. The day before, the sight of withering plum blossoms reminded him of the disgraced lady, so he sent for her and spent the night in her company. Somehow the Honored Consort found out about this and burst in first thing in the morning to make a scene. As the Plum Consort was hiding just behind the curtain, he could hardly summon her from the eastern palace. After a pause, the emperor said, "I have had nothing to do with the Plum Consort since she moved out to the eastern palace."

"But your affection for her still remains, doesn't it?" Lady Yang said angrily, after a quick glance around the room. "Otherwise, where did these come from?" She pointed to some jewelry by the pillow and a pair of lady's shoes under the bed. She walked over to the bed, took the jade hairpin in her hand, and scrutinized it. "If Your Majesty does not leave for the morning audience now, the ministers would surely blame me

for the delay! I dare not offend them in such a way! Please leave to attend the audience, and I will be here waiting for your return!"

Much chagrined, Emperor Xuanzong went back to bed and closed his eyes. "I am not feeling well today. There will be no audience this morning. You'd better leave now, Honored Consort!"

Lady Yang, flushing with anger, stormed out of the room.

Lady Yang, named Yuhuan, had been a consort of Emperor Xuanzong's son Li Mao. Informed of her incomparable beauty, Emperor Xuanzong had her conducted into the palace, and soon conferred on her the title Honored Consort. She was a plump woman with glossy black hair, rosy cheeks, and creamy skin. The charm of her physical beauty was enhanced by her accomplishments in singing, dancing and playing various musical instruments.

Emperor Xuanzong was a music lover himself, and Lady Yang's talents in this respect heightened his infatuation for her. He once composed a piece of music called "Garments of Plumes and Rainbow," which he considered his favorite. Lady Yang could dance with such grace and allure to the accompaniment of this music that she created a fantastical dreamland for the emperor. The emperor was convinced that she was the only person who truly understood his music and who had the gift to expound its meaning with superb dance movements.

Lady Yang's musical talents were not restricted to interpretation. Even the court musicians rarely matched her skills in playing the *pipa* (a four-string instrument) and the chimes. At Emperor Xuanzong's order, precious green jade was gathered from Lantian and made into chimes for Lady Yang. Pleased, she wrote a song titled "Liangzhou," which became quite popular all over the empire.

With her unrivaled beauty, intelligence and talent, Lady Yang soon established herself in the good graces of the emperor. However, her intense jealousy and sometimes fiery temper gave rise to quite a few skirmishes between her and her imperial master.

On one occasion Emperor Xuanzong was so outraged by Lady Yang's irreverent behavior that he ordered the head eunuch, Gao Lishi, to take her back home. However, the deprivation of her company soon proved unbearable for him. As the days went on he grew very restless and irritable. Learning of His Majesty's displeasure, the cooks prepared special dishes for his supper, but the emperor merely glanced at them and ordered them taken away. He was in such a bad mood that he had several attendants whipped for minor offenses.

Aware of the real cause of the emperor's displeasure, Gao Lishi went away and returned with the Honored Consort, who knelt before the emperor to beg his forgiveness. At the very sight of her, Emperor Xuanzong forgot all his worries. After that, Lady Yang received even greater devotion from her imperial master.

Later, Lady Yang suffered another disgrace by being sent home because of her gross indiscretion.

Emperor Xuanzong had deep affection for his brothers and often let them stay the night in his own bedchamber. At that time Lady Yang was a thirtyish woman at the height of her womanly charms and passions, whereas the emperor was over thirty years her senior. She rejoiced at the chance of meeting the princes and soon developed an intimate relation-ship with them. The Prince of Ning, who was highly accomplished in music as well as in horsemanship and archery, roused in her something more than sisterly affection. This enraged Emperor Xuanzong so much that she was again driven out of the palace.

Her cousin, Chief Minister Yang Guozhong, was greatly upset, not knowing whether she could get away with it or not, as she had the previous time. His position in the imperial court and the power and prestige enjoyed by the entire Yang family would vaporize if Lady Yang should fall out of favor with the emperor permanently. However, Yang Guozhong was certain that the emperor could not bear to have his favorite executed. Therefore he told the emperor, "If the Honored Consort, because of her offense, deserves death, please allow her to die in the palace and save her the disgrace of dying outside."

Emperor Xuanzong, torn between conflicting emotions, was deeply affected by these words. He immediately sent an envoy to visit Lady Yang.

When the envoy arrived, Lady Yang burst into tears. She cut a lock of her beautiful black hair and presented it to him, saying, "I am guilty of a grave offense and deserve to die. All that I possess, except for my humble body, has been bestowed by His Majesty. I can offer nothing else but this lock of hair to show my gratitude for his unbounded favor. Let this be my farewell gift!"

When the envoy returned with the lock of hair, Emperor Xuanzong was so alarmed that he sent Gao Lishi to bring Lady Yang back to the palace at once. At the moment of their reunion, he felt too overcome with emotion to say a single word of chastisement. To celebrate the happy reconciliation the emperor lavished gifts on the Yang family.

Lady Yang was fond of litchi, especially those cultivated in a southern regions far away from the capital. To ensure the freshness of the fruits Emperor Xuanzong had them transported by the imperial postal service. The best horses were used in relays along the road; many of them dieing of exhaustion in the process.

The hot summer days often found Emperor Xuanzong and his favorite at Huaqing Palace in the outskirts of the imperial capital, where Lady Yang was wont to bathe herself in the hot spring pond. In the coolness of the evening, she would perform an exquisite dance under the moon, much to the emperor's delight.

The seventh night of the seventh lunar month was the happy moment when the legendary Cowherd and Weaving Girl, a heavenly couple separated by the Milky Way, enjoyed their annual reunion. Gazing into the starlit sky, Lady Yang said, "The Cowherd and the Weaving Girl meet only once a year, but their mutual love has have lasted through the ages. I wonder if Your Majesty's love for me will remain undiminished and everlasting."

Emperor Xuanzong broke into a smile. "We will spend all our living days together, and will be buried in the same grave. Don't you think that is everlasting enough?" He took the beauty by her hand and walked her to the incense burner, where he made a solemn pledge: "May our love last forever like that between the Cowherd and the Weaving Girl, and may the two of us be joined as husband and wife after life!"

"With the stars as witnesses," Lady Yang added hastily, "We have made this pledge. Whoever breaks it shall be punished by heaven!" She turned to face the emperor. "I am infinitely grateful to Your Majesty for making this secret covenant with me. I will stick to it no matter what happens!"

"We share the same feeling," Emperor Xuanzong assured her, giving her an amorous look. "No more worries for you!"

In autumn Emperor Xuanzong returned to the imperial palace with Lady Yang. Singing, dancing and sumptuous feasts remained the order of the day. While enjoying the peonies in the imperial garden with her, the emperor sent for the great poet Li Bai to write in commemoration of the joyous occasion. Impressed by the matchless beauty of the Honored Consort, Li Bai wrote three immortal poems in her praise.

Throughout history few women in the imperial harem could aspire to the fame and favor enjoyed by Yang Yuhuan. However, the blissful days did not last forever. In 755 an armed revolt was raised by An Lushan, a general of Turkish origin. Emperor Xuanzong was taken completely by surprise. The combat power of the imperial troops had declined steadily during the peaceful years, so that the rebels marched from victory to victory toward the capital.

Formerly, quite a few courtiers had doubted An Lushan's loyalty. Yang Guozhong, who had no sympathy for him, had often spoken to the emperor of An's covert maneuvers in preparation for revolt, but the emperor refused to believe him, Yang then went out of his way to make things difficult for An Lushan. When the rebellion finally broke out, no one in the imperial court could devise a strategy for pacifying it.

A capable general named Geshu Han was dispatched to guard the strategic city of Tongguan against the oncoming rebels. Conversant in the art of war, Geshu Han decided to avoid engagement with the enemy. He believed that the rebels, tired by their long march and lacking provisions, would seek a quick battle. If they failed to capture the city in a short time, they would grow discouraged and restless. By launching a counter-attack at this point, the Tang army would surely rout the enemy. Geshu Han's plan seemed impeccable, but he failed to take into account an enemy from within. Yang Guozhong, who bore a deep grudge against the general, spoke ill of him to the emperor. "Geshu Han cowers before the rebels although he has two hundred thousand troops under his command. Why should we maintain such a large army if it doesn't give battle? With the rebels growing in strength from day to day, our troops will fall prey to them soon!"

The witless emperor was thus induced to order Geshu Han to sally out on a counterattack against the rebels, with disastrous results. The imperial troops were annihilated, and Geshu Han surrendered to An Lushan. The gateway to the imperial capital was forced open.

The emperor summoned all his courtiers for an emergency meeting. Some requested him to lead an expedition in person to subjugate the rebels. Others advised him to order the regional commanders to come to his rescue. Yang Guozhong argued that the rebels were too strong to be repelled. In his opinion, the emperor should evacuate the capital and take refuge in the mountains of Sichuan, where he could organize the local troops to recapture the capital. The aged emperor felt no inclination to confront the rebels himself. Escorted by a band of imperial troops, he left for Sichuan in the company of his Honored Consort, Yang Guozhong, and a few courtiers.

Arriving at Mawei a few days later Emperor Xuanzong decided to take a much-needed rest. All of a sudden loud battle-cries rose from the ranks of the escorting army. Sensing a mutiny, both the emperor and his Honored Consort turned pale with fright.

The mutiny was staged by a general named Chen Xuanli, who regarded Yang Guozhong as the main culprit in plunging the empire into chaos. "Yang Guozhong is a traitor!" cried his soldiers in unison. An arrow flew at the chief minister and landed on the saddle of his horse. Yang Guozhong tried to flee, but was caught and killed. Lady Yang's two sisters were dispatched in the same fashion.

The residence of the emperor was then encircled by troops clamoring for justice. Fighting back his fear, Emperor Xuanzong sent his trusted eunuch, Gao Lishi, to negotiate with Chen Xuanli. On his return Gao Lishi said, "Yang Guozhong has been killed, and the Honored Consort can no longer stay. Your Majesty has to surrender her!"

"Why?" Emperor Xuanzong demanded. "The Honored Consort has lived in the rear palace and never meddled in state affairs. Why should she be blamed for the present crisis?"

"The Honored Consort is indeed innocent," agreed Gao Lishi. "However, the troops have killed Yang Guozhong, so they will not feel secure as long as his cousin is by your side. Please consider it, my lord! If the troops feel insecure, how can they ensure your safety?"

Emperor Xuanzong did not reply at once and sent Gao Lishi away. He paced up and down the room, supported on his stick, as his mind flashed back to the days and nights of felicity he had shared with his beloved, and to the secret vow made under the moon on that double seventh night. How could he bring himself to part with her in this way?

Just then Gao Lishi burst in hurriedly. "Your Majesty!" he cried in a panicky voice. "The soldiers have entered the house! They are coming to kill the Honored Consort!"

With a shudder Emperor Xuanzong realized there was no way he could save his favorite. He had no hope of regaining control of his troops unless he gave in to their demand. "I never thought it would come to this!" he grumbled, almost too choked to speak. "Oh well, let the Honored Consort take her own life!" The last words were accompanied by an outpouring of tears.

Lady Yang was trembling in fear over her cousin's death when Gao Lishi came in with the emperor's edict. The shock proved too much for the poor lady, and she passed out. When she came to, tears streamed down her cheeks. "Let me say farewell to His Majesty!"

Struggling her way to Emperor Xuanzong, Lady Yang sobbed uncontrollably, unable to say a word. She could not understand why the soldiers should hate her so much, and why her imperial master could not save her. Listening to the clamor of voices demanding her death, she knew there was no escape for her. Suppressing her grief, she gazed into Emperor Xuanzong's eyes. "I will die without regrets if Your Majesty can take care of himself!" Then she followed Gao Lishi out of the room.

At the news of her death the mutinous troops uttered thunderous cheers. Chen Xuanli took off his suit of armor and pleaded guilty to Emperor Xuanzong, who comforted the general with kind words. After the body of the Honored Consort was buried at the foot of the hill, the emperor and his entourage continued their journey to Sichuan.

When the rebellion was finally subdued, Emperor Xuanzong returned to the imperial capital, Chang'an. His third son had by this time ascended the throne, giving him the title Emperor Emeritus. The scenery in the palace was as lovely as before, but the incomparable beauty was gone forever. Feelings of everlasting regret and sorrow accompanied the old man until his death.

THE GREEDY EMPRESS LIU

The end of the Tang Dynasty was followed by an unstable period known as the Five Dynasties (907-960). Li Chunmao, the ruler of the state of Jin, not only achieved military exploits but was also accomplished in the letters and music.

One day the young sovereign paid a visit to his mother, Lady Cao, who gave a grand feast in his honor with several young maidens performing songs and dances. One of them, Liu Jingui, attracted his attention. She had a pretty face, lovely figure, and crystal-clear singing voice. A few of her songs were followed by her playing a wind pipe and a drum, instruments on which she performed with great dexterity.

His eyes glued to the young maiden, Li Chunmao was profuse in his praise for her. Deferring to her son's infatuation, Lady Cao gave the maiden to him as a gift.

Li Chunmao took her back and allocated an entire compound to be her residence. Soon after, she bore him a son. Finding a strong likeness in the boy to himself, Li Chunmao doted on the lad and showed increasing partiality toward Liu Jingui, who thereby became his favorite among the various consorts. For over ten years of continuous military campaigns, Li Chunmao always took her in his company. By virtue of her intelligence, artifices, and tender solicitude, she made herself an indispensable asset of her sovereign, whose other consorts seldom got a chance to wait on him.

Liu Jingui had been taken away from her family by force at the age of six. Her father, Liu Shanren, was drifting from place to place when he learned of his daughter's good fortune, so he presented himself at the palace to request a meeting with his daughter. Li Chunmao sent for the officer who had brought Li Jingui into the palace and asked him if anyone else had been present when he seized the girl. "Yes," the officer replied. "There was a yellow-bearded old man." When Liu Shanren was brought in, the officer identified him.

Unfortunately the old man chose an inopportune time to barge in on his daughter. Liu Jingui and a few consorts competing for Li Chunmao's favor were at that time trying to outdo one another by claiming noble descent. It would be unthinkable for her to acknowledge a poorly dressed, shrunken old man as her father. "As far as I remember," she said, "my father died at the hands of bandits. I wept bitterly over his body. After that I left my hometown. What is this old man doing here?" To prove that she had nothing to do with the old man, she had her father whipped at the palace gate and driven away.

In 922 Li Chunmao proclaimed himself emperor of the Later Tang Dynasty. In the following ten years he launched a series of campaigns against rival states until they were wiped out. At the age of thirty-eight, he became the supreme ruler of China. His ambitions fulfilled, he considered it a good idea to devote his attention to his favorite pastime. The imperial palace became the site of endless merry-making. A lover of songs and music, he showed a special taste for opera. The palace attendants had to gather for frequent rehearsals, in which the emperor himself played a part. This enabled Liu Jingui, now the empress, to take control of the court.

A woman of humble origin, Liu Jingui attributed her miraculous rise to power to Buddha's blessing and she became a devout Buddhist, although she did not eschew sensual pleasures for this sake. Her greatest passion was accumulating wealth, perhaps due to her childhood memories of the horror of poverty. She sent out envoys to do business in the name of the imperial palace, dictating whatever terms suited them best. Such a practice proved quite successful, bringing an endless flow of money into Empress Liu's private coffer.

Another source of her income was tributes from the court

and local officials, whose careers depended solely on the favor of the emperor. Some of them, recognizing Empress Liu's influence, curried favor with her by offering her handsome gifts. The empress was immensely pleased, and the emperor did not raise any objection. The vast accumulation of wealth afforded Empress Liu infinite delight. Her days were spent in copying Buddhist scriptures to distribute among the monasteries. Under her influence, Li Chunmao also became a Buddhist.

Li Chunmao's passion for opera gave Empress Liu a chance to consolidate her position at court. The talented performers she selected to wait on the emperor became increasingly powerful. With their assistance she held great sway over the imperial court.

The Dynasty went on a rapid course of decline. The emperor's partiality toward a bunch of performers and his indifference toward his meritorious generals caused widespread discontent. Because of the excessive greed of the empress, officers and men of the imperial army often went without salary. In contrast, the empress herself did not practice frugality but chose to live in great extravagance.

To relieve the monotony of palace life, Li Chunmao and his empress began to take long excursions. The troops forming their escort, with their salaries badly in arrears, barely had enough to eat or wear, and some of them committed robberies in broad daylight. An atmosphere of uncertainty and pending disaster loomed over the empire.

Many courtiers grew anxious and petitioned the emperor to dole out some money to appease his troops. Li Chunmao told Empress Liu to open the imperial treasury, but in vain. When the chief minister came again to urge the emperor to pay his troops, Empress Liu overheard everything from behind a curtain. Picking up a few pieces of jewelry, she showed them to the emperor. "All the articles of tribute from the vassal lords have been used up. These are the only valuables left in the palace. You can give them to the soldiers!" Li Chunmao did not refute her, and the chief minister went away in despair.

Soon afterward a mutiny broke out. Li Chunmao decided to lead an expedition in person against the mutineers and offered high rewards to the troops. "By the time we get the money, our families will have starved to death!" clamored the angry soldiers. After promising to distribute an incoming tax payment of half a million tales of silver to the army, the emperor managed to gather together twenty-five thousand men, with which he set out.

Halfway along the journey, when they had to tread a difficult mountain path, more than half of the soldiers deserted. The emperor sent his close followers to stop the deserters, saying, "When the half a million taels of silver arrives, the entire amount will be distributed among you!" But the soldiers were unimpressed. "His Majesty's money will come too late! Even those who stay to receive it will not be thankful!"

Li Chunmao turned to the overseer of the palace storehouse for help. "There is really nothing left," the overseer replied. Some soldiers were so enraged on hearing this that they drew their swords to kill the overseer, saying, "It is people like you who have ruined our empire!" The overseer, though saved by the intervention of the emperor's guards, sank into despair. "Empress Liu won't pay the troops because she wants to keep all the wealth for herself. And it is I who gets the blame for it! If something goes wrong, I will die a cruel death, with my body torn into pieces!" He went away and drowned himself in the river.

Shortly afterward a group of soldiers attempted to assassinate the emperor. They failed and were executed. Li Chunmao gave the general in charge such a severe thrashing that the general raised a revolt himself. Caught by surprise, Li Chunmao suffered fatal injuries in the entangled fight. Two arrows were planted in his chest.

While the dying emperor longed to bid farewell to his empress, her hands were full with something more urgent. She was busily collecting her hoarded valuables to take away with her. Finally Li Chunmao died of the excessive loss of blood, and Empress Liu fled the capital with her fortune. With no place to go, she took the veil at a nunnery, in the hope that Buddha would enable her to spend the rest of her life in peace and comfort.

After pacification of the mutiny, a new emperor was chosen. He regarded Empress Liu as the scourge of the nation, and her greed the source of the bloody turmoils. He had a band of soldiers hunt her out and force her to commit suicide.

EMPRESS LIU AND HER LUCKLESS MAID

Emperor Zhenzong of the Song Dynasty (reigned 997-1022) had a capable empress, Lady Liu. Intelligent and well-educated, she showed a remarkable ability to deal with state affairs. After his daily audience, Emperor Zhenzong often retired to his residence to read the memorials of his ministers late into the night. On such occasions he always had Empress Liu for company, and she proved an able assistant. Whenever something happened in the rear palace, Empress Liu would deal with it according to established rules and precedents, without bothering the emperor. Thus Emperor Zhenzong treated her with both love and respect and never failed to consult her on important issues at the imperial court.

Toward the end of his reign Emperor Zhenzong suddenly came down with a grave illness. Unable to preside over the court anymore, he delegated most of his power to Empress Liu. His courtiers, however, preferred a provisional rule by the crown prince. With great reluctance, Empress Liu gave in to them.

A year later Emperor Zhenzong died. The crown prince ascended the throne, to be known in history as Emperor Renzong (reigned 1022-1062). At thirteen the emperor was too young to hold court independently, so Lady Liu, as the empress dowager, attended his audiences behind a curtain. By employing both kindness and severity she kept even the most unruly ministers at bay. By her arrangement the emperor, when he was not holding court, had some renowned scholars teach him history and the Confucian classics.

One day Empress Dowager Liu asked a trusted minister, "What do you think of Empress Wu Zetian of the Tang

Dynasty?" The answer was unequivocal. "She was a scourge of the nation who nearly toppled the Tang empire." Lady Liu fell silent. She admired Wu Zetian and was keen to follow her example. Unfortunately even her most trusted courtiers showed no inclination to encourage her.

A few years later Lady Li, a consort of the late Emperor Zhenzong died in the palace. Empress Dowager Liu had no intention of publicizing the matter and wanted to have the woman buried quietly. However, the ministers would not allow this. At the morning audience one day Chief Minister Lü Yijian said to Lady Liu, "I heard a palace woman died recently. Is this true?" The empress dowager burst into a rage. "Why should the chief minister meddle into the affairs of the rear palace?" With this she dismissed the audience and dragged Emperor Renzong out of the hall.

Lady Liu did not feel offended without reason. The dead palace woman was in fact the birth mother of the ruling emperor.

Lady Li used to be a maid servant of Empress Liu sent to oversee Emperor Zhenzong's everyday sleep. Enchanted by her lovely person and quiet, modest manners, the emperor often had her spend the night with him. Finally she became pregnant, and the delighted Emperor Zhenzong spent more and more time in her company.

On a fine day Lady Li and Emperor Zhenzong were enjoying the scenery from a terrace when a jade pin slipped out of her hair and dropped down to the ground below. She was upset, perceiving it as a bad omen, but the emperor smiled and ordered an attendant to bring up the pin. He prayed silently, "If the pin is not broken, that means she will bear me a son." When the pin was brought to him intact, he went into rapture much to the puzzlement of Lady Li and the attendants.

Shortly afterward Lady Li gave birth to a son. The entire palace rejoiced that the emperor, hitherto sonless, was at last blessed with an heir. Only then did he tell Lady Li about his silent prayer.

Immediately after the baby's birth Empress Liu took the baby away and brought him up as her own son. The boy, named Zhao Zhen, received solicitous care from Empress Liu, never knowing who his natural mother was. Nor did the palace attendants, who knew the secret, dare mention it to him for fear of offending the empress.

After Emperor Zhenzong's death, Zhao Zhen succeeded to the throne as Emperor Renzong. Lady Liu was elevated to empress dowager. Lady Li lived on in obscurity for some years. She had to swallow her humiliation and keep silent about her identity to protect herself from the jealous Empress Dowager Liu. Finally she received the title Chamber Consort for her submissive conduct.

Ten years after her son's ascension to the throne Lady Li died, to the immense relief of Empress Dowager Liu. In her opinion, Lady Li had gained everything she could ever hope for: the late emperor's favor, the bearing of an imperial heir, and the title of imperial consort. What else could a former maid servant have expected? Therefore she intended to have Lady Li's funeral conducted in the manner befitting her rank of Chamber Consort. But the objection of the courtiers was hard for her to ignore.

A few days later Empress Dowager Liu sent for Lü Yijian and asked him, "Why should you show so much concern over the death of a palace woman?"

"As Chief Minister," Lü replied, "I have a duty to attend to all affairs both inside and outside the palace."

"Are you trying to sow discord between me and my son?" demanded Lady Liu.

"I would not have spoken about the matter if I were not thinking about your future," Lü Yijian responded. "If you hope to be honored and respected after you are gone, you must have Lady Li's funeral executed in a most grand fashion!"

Empress Dowager Liu suddenly saw the light. "What arrangement would be appropriate then?" she asked.

Lü Yijian advised her to bury Lady Li like an official of the first rank, second only to the empress. She should be dressed in the empress dowager's robes and placed in a mercury coffin.

A year later Empress Dowager Liu died. Only then was Emperor Renzong informed of his true descent. He learned that his mother, Lady Li, died a cruel death after suffering numerous humiliations and was buried in the most perfunctory fashion. Emperor Renzong's anguish knew no bounds. He immediately promulgated an edict blaming himself for unfilial behavior. Then he ordered Lady Li's coffin to be opened to ascertain the cause of her death. When the coffin was opened, Emperor Renzong and the attendants stared in disbelief. The coffin, of high-quality wood and superb craftsmanship, was filled with mercury. Lady Li's body was well-preserved; she looked peaceful and serene, and her visage showed a lifelike color. Moreover, she was dressed in robes befitting an empress dowager. Convinced of the benign nature of his foster mother, Emperor Renzong said with a deep sigh that rumors were indeed not to be trusted. Thus the late Empress Dowager Liu continued to be honored, and her family remained in the good graces of the emperor.

EMPRESS MA,
A PARAGON OF BENEVOLENCE

More often than not the founding emperor of a new dynasty had a capable wife who shared his weal and woe while he fought his way to the throne. Zhu Yuanzhang, the first emperor of the Ming Dynasty (reigned 1368-1398), had exactly such a wife, Empress Ma.

At an early age she had been entrusted by her father to a wealthy friend of his, Guo Zixing. Shortly afterwards her father died, and Guo adopted her as his own daughter. A sensible and intelligent girl, she won the good graces of both Guo and his wife.

Zhu Yuanzhang, the future Ming emperor, was a native of Haozhou. A severe famine wreaked havoc in his hometown when he was seventeen. With most of his family members starving to death, Zhu wandered from place to place until Guo Zixing, impressed with his strong physique and stentorian voice, received him into his household.

Whatever task was assigned to him, Zhu Yuanzhang never failed to carry it out prudently, thus Guo Zixing became very fond of him and let him become his son-in-law.

By that time Guo's adopted daughter had grown into a lovely young maiden. The charm of her natural beauty was enhanced by her unassuming manners. The two were married, and Zhu Yuanzhang, who was then virtually illiterate, held his well-educated wife in great respect.

Aware of her husband's aspirations, Lady Ma tried to induce him to devote some attention to study. Zhu was given to understand that a good knowledge of history and geography would further his career. After a short time he made such progress in his studies that he could compose poems to convey his feelings.

Toward the end of the Yuan Dynasty the Mongol rulers were losing control of the empire. By enlisting talented people under his service and building a power base of his own, Zhu Yuanzhang gradually grew independent of Guo Zixing, whose suspicion and jealousy rose with each passing day.

Sensing his precarious position, Zhu turned to his wife for help. Lady Ma advised him to treat Guo with more humility and deliver most of his spoils to him. In the meantime she called on her foster mother and asked her to speak to Guo in favor of Zhu Yuanzhang. In this way Zhu was saved from many troubles.

However, Guo Zixing's son bore a deep grudge against Zhu Yuanzhang. Once, he had Zhu locked up in a room and forbade anyone to send him food or drink. When Lady Ma paid her husband a visit she tucked a few newly steamed pancakes into her bosom, which enabled him to live through the ordeal. But her bosom was singed by the heat.

When Guo Zixing died, Zhu Yuanzhang took control of his troops at the age of twenty-eight. Whenever he conquered an area he won widespread support of the local people by abolishing the oppressive laws of the Mongols. At lady Ma's suggestion he sought out some renowned hermits and made them his military advisors.

Zhu Yuanzhang finally wiped out all the Yuan forces and defeated all his other military rivals. With China reunified, he set himself up as emperor and founded the Ming Dynasty. Lady Ma was made empress.

In attending to the affairs of the rear palace Empress Ma strived to educate the numerous palace women in the ancient rules of propriety. In her opinion the Song Dynasty had many virtuous empresses, so she compiled a collection of their sayings for everyday consultation. Once, someone remarked to her that the Song empresses showed an excess of benevolence. To this Empress Ma rejoined, "Isn't that more preferable than an excess of malignancy?"

After becoming empress Lady Ma continued to oversee the everyday needs of her husband and always checked his meal herself. When the attendants told her it was unnecessary for her to attend to such matters in person, she replied that it was the duty of a wife to take good care of her husband. Moreover, with her supervising the kitchen, if the emperor should ever find fault with his food, no palace attendant would be held responsible.

On one occasion an attending maid committed an offense that infuriated the emperor. Empress Ma also feigned indignation and ordered her to be handed over to the Palace Surveillance Office. Later, Zhu Yuanzhang asked her to explain her reaction. Empress Ma replied, "An emperor must not impose rewards or punishments according to his likes or dislikes. When you are in a rage, the punishment you mete out can be inappropriately severe. If the case is tried by the Palace Surveillance Office instead, a just verdict will be ensured. Likewise, in the prosecution of officials, it is better to leave the matter to relevant departments of the government."

One day Zhu Yuanzhang summoned some of his ministers for a meeting in the main hall of the palace. A bit later he sent for a meal. At this juncture Empress Ma came and had the food for the ministers brought to her. After tasting it, she found the food cold and flavorless, and she did not hesitate to point this out to the emperor. "Every sage ruler in ancient times practiced frugality himself but treated men of talent with generosity. But I just found the food prepared for the court officials to be cold and tasteless. This is perhaps not the proper way to treat talent!" At her words, the court officials present were filled with admiration.

Because of his quick temper Zhu Yuanzhang sometimes tended to make rash decisions. On such occasions Empress Ma tried her best to dissuade him. Zhu Yuanzhang had a trusted minister named Guo Jingxiang. When someone accused Guo's son of plotting to assassinate his father, Zhu Yuanzhang flew into a rage and intended to have Guo's son executed at once, but Empress Ma stopped him. "This is the only son Guo Jingxiang has. If he should be killed by mistake, the Guo family would be left without an heir!" Zhu Yuanzhang ordered an investigation into the case and found Guo's son innocent.

A general named Li Wenzhong was the garrison commander of Yanzhou, a strategic border region. When someone accused him of wrongdoing, Zhu Yuanzhang decided to call him back to the capital and give him a severe reprimand. Again Empress Ma intervened. "As Yanzhou is a strategic region bordering on a hostile state, the decision to change its commander should not be made so lightly. For years Li Wenzhong has displayed his honesty, competence, and devotion to Your Majesty. Why should you believe the charge against him without obtaining further proof?" Zhu Yuanzhang thereupon agreed to put the matter aside. Later Li Wenzhong bore out Empress Ma's words by achieving great merits.

As the city walls of the imperial capital needed to be renovated, a wealthy man named Shen Xiu offered to help. Zhu Yuanzhang agreed to let him undertake half of the project, with the other half to be conducted by the government. A deadline was set for the completion of the construction work. It turned out that Shen Xiu did an excellent job and finished his share three days before the government did. Feeling affronted, Zhu Yuanzhang wanted to find an excuse to put Shen Xiu to death. When Empress Ma spoke to him in Shen Xiu's favor, he refused to listen. "It is a bad omen for a commoner to have greater wealth than the government!" he grumbled indignantly.

Empress Ma reasoned with him patiently. "The law of the empire has been established to punish a man for his misdeeds, not for being a bad omen." Unable to refute her, Zhu Yuanzhang agreed to spare Shen Xiu's life.

One day Empress Ma asked her husband, "Are people living in peace and contentment?"

"This is not a question you should ask," replied Zhu Yuanzhang.

"Your Majesty is the imperial father of his subjects, and I am their imperial mother. Isn't it natural for a mother to show concern over the welfare of her children?"

When the nation suffered a drought, Empress Ma would abstained from meat together with her attendants and prayed to heaven. If a famine broke out, she would eat simple meals like those served in an ordinary household. Zhu Yuanzhang told her she need not practice frugality in such a manner, for the government was collecting grains to relieve the famine victims. "Instead of gathering grains after a famine has broken out," she said, "it would be better to store them during bumper years in case of such an emergency."

It was customary for the generals on their return from successful expeditions against the Mongols to bring their spoils of victory to the imperial palace. Looking at these heaps of treasure, Empress Ma remarked to Zhu Yuanzhang, "The people of Yuan were in possession of so much treasure, yet they failed to keep it. I hope Your Majesty has in his possession something more precious."

Zhu Yuanzhang realized at once what she meant. "I guess you are talking about men of virtue and talent," he said.

"Yes," replied Empress Ma. "With what we have achieved today, it is easy to forget about our humble past. Luxury and comfort engenders pride and corruption; indiscretion in small matters may result in the downfall of our empire. I hope Your Majesty will spare no effort to obtain men of virtue and talent and have them assist him in governing the empire."

On another occasion Empress Ma said, "If the legal system of a nation is incomplete, a bunch of evil-doers will take the chance to wreak havoc on innocent people. If the common people cannot live and work in peace, they will be forced to rise up in revolt." "This is a golden saying!" Zhu Yuanzhang exclaimed in admiration, and had her words recorded in his memoirs.

In autumn of the fifteenth year of the Hongwu reign (1382) Empress Ma became acutely ill. The ministers suggested that sacrifices be offered to heaven and the best physicians be brought into the palace to treat her. Empress Ma declined. "A person's life span is determined by fate," she said to Zhu Yuanzhang. "What good can a sacrifice do? Besides, even the best physicians of the empire cannot save someone destined to die. If the medicine they prescribe fails to cure me, wouldn't they be incriminated for my sake?"

On her deathbed Empress Ma was asked by Zhu Yuanzhang to speak her last words. "I hope that Your Majesty will enlist men of virtue and talent into his service, accept the advice of his honest courtiers, and enable his loyal subjects to be free from want." With this she closed her eyes forever. She died at the age of fifty-one.

The palace was overcast in an atmosphere of deep sorrow at the death of Empress Ma. The court officials and even the common people sincerely mourned for her. Zhu Yuanzhang was overwhelmed with grief and decided never to name another empress.

LADY WANG'S ASSASSINATION
ATTEMPT AGAINST
THE EMPEROR

Emperor Shizong of the Ming Dynasty (reigned 1521-1566), like many imperial rulers of China, had an intense craving for immortality. Once a courtier introduced to him an eighty-year-old Taoist priest. Though silver-haired, the Taoist had a youthful complexion and walked at a brisk pace. Emperor Shizong could hardly wait to learn the secret of his youth.

The Taoist disclosed that he was in the habit of drinking dewdrops in the early morning. This had the function of invigorating his vital energy, cleaning the stomach and intestines, and clearing his chest. Delighted, Emperor Shizong ordered the palace maids to collect dewdrops in the imperial garden every day to serve as his morning drink.

Thereafter forty maids gathered in the garden at dawn each day. Holding jade cups in their left hands, they used pairs of jade chopsticks to gather dewdrops from the tree leaves which had been washed clean the previous day. Their robes dampened by the dew, the maids shuddered in the cool morning breeze. By drinking the dew together with ginseng soup and other herbal concoctions, Emperor Shizong began to glow with energy. Thus dew gathering became a regular task of the palace maids.

Worn down by this cruel regimen, some palace maids fell ill, and the rest seethed with discontent. Due to the influence of the various concoctions he was consuming, Emperor Shizong became quite irritable and often found excuses to have the palace maids whipped. Gathering dew in the morning became a punishment he meted out to misbehaving consorts and palace maids.

Emperor Shizong had a favored consort, Lady Wang. Though not a ravishing beauty, she knew how to ingratiate herself by attending to the emperor's various needs and caprices. One of her trump cards was the recitation of lines from Emperor Shizong's favorite poems. In spite of all that, appearance still mattered the most for a consort. Thus Emperor Shizong eventually became attached to Lady Cao, titled the Upright Consort, who was exceedingly beautiful. Naturally Lady Wang, the other consorts and even the empress became green with envy.

Now that she enjoyed the emperor's exclusive favor, Lady Cao grew increasingly arrogant and irreverent toward her peers, so much so that she sometimes reproached them at the dinner table. Filled with indignation, Lady Wang often cursed her rival in private. Unfortunately Lady Cao, who had many informants in the palace, soon learned of this. In a rage she complained to the emperor, telling a much embellished story of Lady Wang's incivility. Emperor Shizong immediately had Lady Wang whipped and sent to gather morning dew.

Among the dew-gathering maids Yang Jinying and Xing Cuilian were both nearly thirty years old. Cashing in on their seniority, they ordered the younger maids to gather dew while they lay in bed pleading illness. When their trick was exposed, they were punished with a severe flogging and the unending task of dew gathering. While the other maids were organized in three-day shifts, the two of them had to do it day after day. For minor offences they were flogged again and again. Lady Wang felt sympathy for her fellow sufferers and made friends with them. They often met to air their grievances. Company in distress seemed to make their trouble a little less unbearable. Later, the little group were joined by Zhang Jinlian and Wang Xiulan. As their sympathy grew for one another, their hatred for Emperor Shizong intensified.

Emperor Shizong was aided in his quest for immortality

by many Taoist priests, who kept offering him auspicious animals and plants such as the white crane, snow deer, and various divine herbs. One of them painted a tortoise in five colors and presented it to the emperor, claiming it to be a thousand-year-old divine animal. Delighted, Emperor Shizong had the tortoise placed in a pond and often went to see it in the company of his consorts. Yang Jinying and Xing Cuilian received the thankless task of looking after the divine animal.

Some days later the five-color tortoise died. Yang and Xing were terrified, knowing the enraged emperor would certainly punish them with death. Hastily they went to seek help from Lady Wang. After recovering from the initial shock, she thought for a moment, then said calmly, "Now that it has come to this, we'd better strike first. Why not fight our way out instead of waiting to be killed?"

"But how do we fight our way out?" they asked.

"Every day the dewdrops we gather in the morning are taken to the Imperial Kitchen, where the cooks steam them under the supervision of Upright Consort Cao. At that hour the emperor is fast asleep, and no one would dare disturb him. After Cao has left for the kitchen, there will be only two attendants in the room. When I send them away on some excuse, the two of you can walk in and strangle the emperor with a rope. In the alarm and commotion caused by the emperor's sudden death, the five-color tortoise will be totally forgotten!"

The two maids were flabbergasted. It would be unthinkable for them to assassinate the emperor. Yet, on second thought, they agreed that it was the only way to save their own lives. More people would be needed to ensure the success of the plot, so they talked Zhang Jinlian and Wang Xiulan and asked them to join in the scheme.

On a lovely day in autumn Emperor Shizong busied himself in offering sacrifices to heaven. At nightfall he arrived at Lady Cao's residence, where they drank wine and made love. It was almost daybreak when they both finally went to sleep.

At this juncture Lady Wang, together with Yang Jinying, Xing Cuilian, Zhang Jinlian and Wang Xiulan, brought the dewdrops they had gathered to the imperial kitchen, then went stealthily to Lady Cao's residence and hid themselves among the flowers. After Lady Cao got up at the usual hour and left for the kitchen, Lady Wang went in and sent away the two attending maids. At her signal, her four conspirators rushed into the room.

As they had expected, the emperor was sound asleep. Yang Jinying took out a silk cord, slipped it around his neck, and pulled with all her might. Xing, Zhang and Wang threw themselves on the emperor, holding down his arms and legs. However, the cord could not be tightened, for in her haste Yang Jinying had made a fast knot. Emperor Shizong woke up and began to struggle for dear life. Yang Jinying tied the end of the cord to a bedpost and threw her weight against it. Emperor Shizong began to gasp for breath, his eyes bulging and his tongue sticking out.

Anxious to dispatch the emperor, Yang Jinying beckoned Xing and Wang to pull the cord in her place, while she put her hands around his throat and tightened her grip. In a flurry to get the deed done, the palace maids did not coordinate well, enabling the emperor to regain his breath and fight back. Zhang Jinlian was the first to take to her heels.

Lady Wang, who had been waiting outside, realized that something was terribly wrong when she saw Zhang Jinlian rushing out. She hastened into the room and told the palace maids to leave at once. All of them followed her advice except Yang Jinying.

Shortly afterward the empress arrived with a few attending maids. At their footsteps Yang Jinying tried to conceal herself, but it was too late. She was caught red-handed.

Entering the room, the empress was staggered by what she

saw. The emperor, tied to the bedpost with a cord, seemed to be breathing his last breath. His hair was dishevelled, his eyes bulged and his tongue stuck out. The empress had the cord untied and sent for the court physician posthaste. She had all the maids arrested and the palace put under heavy surveillance.

Emperor Shizong narrowly survived the incident and had to spend the next two months in bed. During this time the empress ordered a thorough investigation into the case. Lady Wang was found to be the chief conspirator. Knowing she could not escape death, she tried to implicate all her personal enemies, including Upright Consort Lady Cao. As the empress had also been jealous of Lady Cao, she was more than willing to accept the charge against her. Thus Lady Cao, along with Lady Wang, Yang Jinying and a few other palace women were found guilty and executed.

EMPRESS DOWAGER CIXI

Empress Dowager Cixi (1834-1908) was a consort of Emperor Xianfeng (reigned 1851-1862) and the mother of Emperor Tongzhi (reigned 1862-1875).

Her family name was Nala and her maiden name Lan'er. As a child she was unusually bright. When her father taught her to read, he was impressed by her quick mind. She showed special interest in history books and a deep admiration for Empress Lü of Han and Empress Wu Zetian of Tang. Brought up in the south, she acquired all the fine qualities of a southern-type beauty, with a slim figure, fresh countenance, and sweet temper. She further enhanced her charm by her superb skills at self-adornment.

A beauty in full bloom at seventeen, Lan'er was selected to enter the palace to wait on the new emperor. Each day she made up with the utmost care, hoping to capture the emperor's heart. However, she waited for a long time without meeting the emperor even once. A few months after his ascension, Emperor Xianfeng already had appointed numerous consorts, concubines and titled ladies as his lesser wives. An ordinary palace woman like Lan'er had little chance to come near to her imperial master.

Lan'er spared no effort to grab any such chance. Out of her monthly allowance she bribed some eunuchs, from whom she was able to learn the whereabouts of the emperor. By hook and by crook, she cultivated the good will of people around her and ingratiated herself with the empress. Thereby she won great popularity in the rear palace.

It is well said that Providence will not let someone down who has tried his best. One day Lan'er learned from a eunuch that the emperor went to the Qinghua Pavilion for his noon

nap each day. Lan'er jumped with joy at the grand opportunity. From then on she planted herself every day at noon by the path to the Qinghua Pavilion, where she sang among the flowers. The southern ditties that she sang sounded pleasing to Emperor Xianfeng, who ordered the singer brought to him. He fell in love with her at first sight. Compared with his numerous consorts, Lan'er seemed to possess a unusual vigor and freshness.

Though the emperor showed increasing partiality toward her, Lan'er did not lose her head. She was well aware that to gain a foothold in the palace she must ensure that the emperor pay her more than passing notice. When the emperor had her for company, her gentleness and solicitude knew no bounds. Emperor Xianfeng became so attached to her that he began to neglect his other consorts. Entering the palace as an ordinary maid, Lan'er received rapid promotions, first to Worthy Lady, then to Fair Concubine. In 1856 she gave birth to a boy, who was named Zaichun. The only son of Emperor Xianfeng, he was to become Emperor Tongzhi. After this Lan'er received the title Fair Consort, ranking second only to the empress. As mother of the only imperial prince, she enjoyed unrivaled status in the rear palace.

With her position firmly established, Lan'er began to show an intense interest in the affairs of the court. Sometimes she kept the emperor company when he was discussing important issues with his courtiers. As women were strictly forbidden by the imperial law to meddle in state affairs, she was cautious at first, offering a piece of advice only when the emperor desperately needed one. Impressed by her capability, Emperor Xianfeng often consulted her when he was unable to reach a decision about a particular problem. Before long she was poring over memorials presented by court officials and even composing imperial edicts on the emperor's behalf. This enabled her to gain a sound knowledge of the situation inside and outside the court and the imperial laws and regulations.

At the same time she learned many ways to handle the various officials and make them work to her benefit.

Upon his ascension Emperor Xianfeng strived to be a conscientious ruler and tried to save the Qing empire from further decline. Yet he was unable to reverse the tide, and watched on helplessly in the face of internal turmoil and incursions of foreign imperialist powers. In March 1860 the Anglo-French joint forces laid siege to Beijing, the imperial capital. Instead of rallying forces to repel the invaders, Emperor Xianfeng fled to his summer resort in Chengde, together with his courtiers, princes, and consorts. He despaired of ever restoring the empire to its former glory and indulged himself in hunting and excessive merry-making. A few courtiers headed by Sushun and Yixin were put in charge of the daily affairs of the court, and the Fair Consort took over the checking and approving of memorials.

The Fair Consort grew increasingly arrogant and unscrupulous. Sometimes she even wrote instructions in the emperor's name and sent them out without telling him. When the emperor found out about this, he was at first quite irritated. However, as she had made no mistake in her instructions, he did not bother to confront her with her presumption. Troubled by the predominance of the Fair Consort, several courtiers tried to remind the emperor of the perils of letting a woman meddle in state affairs. But the emperor, absorbed in his sensual pursuits, did not feel inclined to intervene.

His health undermined by intemperance, Emperor Xianfeng fell seriously ill in July 1861. On his deathbed he sent for his empress and gave her a secret edict. Then he summoned eight courtiers, including Sushun, Zaiyuan and Duanhua, to whom he consigned Zaichun, the underage crown prince and future sovereign.

The following day Emperor Xianfeng died. His empress received the title Empress Dowager Ci'an, and his Fair Consort, Empress Dowager Cixi. They were also called the Eastern Empress Dowager and the Western Empress Dowager respectively after the relative position of their residences.

Empress Dowager Cixi arranged for a courtier named Dong Yuanchun to send in a memorial requesting the two empresses dowager to hold court from behind curtains. After that, she and Ci'an summoned the eight most trusted courtiers of the late emperor and asked their opinion about Dong's suggestion. "The imperial laws do not prescribe such practice," objected Zaiyuan.

"They do not prescribe it," said Cixi, "but neither do they forbid it. In addition, Dong has suggested that one or two imperial princes be selected to assist in dealing with court affairs. I think the method is practical."

"But the imperial law must be strictly obeyed," rejoined Duanhua. "Anything included in them cannot be repealed, and anything not included cannot be added."

Empress Dowager Cixi frowned. To relieve the tense atmosphere, Ci'an said, "This is a matter of great significance. Maybe you need more time to consider it."

"From what they have said," Cixi said indignantly, "they have no intention at all of carrying out our edict."

Unable to contain his temper, Sushun blurted out, "We have been entrusted to assist the emperor himself, not the empresses dowager. How can we carry out an edict that goes against the established rules?"

Glaring at the unruly courtier, Cixi tried hard not to have an outburst of rage. Again Ci'an did the peacemaking, saying, "There is plenty of time to give the matter careful consideration. Let them leave now."

After that the eight ministers submitted a memorial denouncing Dong Yuanchun's proposal as totally unpracticable, hoping thereby to curb Cixi's ambition.

Yixin, titled Prince of Gong, was Emperor Xianfeng's half-brother. After the occupation of Beijing by the Anglo-

French forces, he negotiated with them on behalf of the Qing government and managed to gain their trust. Priding himself on his abilities and merits, he had no respect for the eight powerful ministers headed by Sushun who, entrusted by the late Emperor Xianfeng to assist his son, defied anyone to challenge their lofty position.

Such tension and strife among the courtiers did not escape the watchful eyes of Empress Dowager Cixi. Neither side had her sympathy, for they were all obstacles to her ambition. But, as a first step, she decided to employ Yixin to get rid of Sushun. Yixin, who grossly underestimated Cixi, accepted her offer of an alliance without hesitation.

In September 1861 Empress Dowager Cixi ordered Sushun to escort Emperor Xianfeng's coffin back to Beijing along the main road. Accompanied by Empress Dowager Ci'an, the new emperor, and other courtiers, she took a shortcut and arrived at the capital ahead of Sushun. On her return, a group of courtiers headed by Jia Zhen presented a joint petition requesting the two empresses dowager to preside over the court. Yixin took the initiative against his enemies by arresting Sushun's allies, Zaiyuan and Duanhua, who had escorted Cixi back to Beijing. Cixi, in the meantime, sent men to seize Sushun and bring him posthaste to Beijing.

Back in Beijing, Sushun was taken to the Court of the Imperial Clan, where he met Zaiyuan and Duanhua. Only then did he realize that he had been totally defeated. He had arranged for Zaiyuan and Duanhua to accompany Cixi in order to assassinate her along the way. However, Cixi had arranged for herself to be protected by a band of imperial guards headed by Rong Lu.

In early October Emperor Xianfeng's coffin arrived in Beijing and was received by the two empresses dowager, the emperor and the court officials, all dressed in mourning. Shortly afterward the new emperor was crowned. An imperial edict was issued that denounced Sushun and his henchmen.

Sushun, Zaiyuan and Duanhua were executed, and their close followers dismissed and exiled. None of the court officials dared challenge Cixi's authority. The reign title of the Qing Dynasty was named Tongzhi (joint-rule), signifying that the two empresses dowager, Cixi and Ci'an, would hold court together.

At the beginning Empress Dowager Cixi proved herself a capable ruler. In affairs of the court she relied heavily on Yixin, who in addition to his abilities befitting a prince and courtier had a flair for diplomacy. Zeng Guofan and Zuo Zongtang, two local officials both of Han instead of Manchu descent, were put to the task of suppressing the uprisings of peasants and ethnic peoples, which they accomplished in a short time. Cixi also encouraged the development of modern industry for military and civil production. In the first part of the Tongzhi reign the country enjoyed relative peace and security.

Cixi treated Ci'an with proper deference at first. Though she attended to the daily affairs of the court, she never failed to consult Ci'an on matters of importance. Though mild in disposition and indifferent to fame and power, Ci'an sometimes intervened when Cixi's conduct did not suit her idea of justice. Thus Cixi began to hold a grudge against her.

Cixi had a trusted eunuch named An Dehai, who kept close watch of the conduct of Emperor Tongzhi and the other courtiers. Relying on Cixi's trust he showed increasing arrogance and lack of scruples. He enlisted his personal adherents among the officials and held increasing sway over the imperial court. Many courtiers bore a biting hatred against him. Empress Dowager Ci'an, learning of the eunuch's excesses, advised Cixi to curb him. This annoyed Cixi, but she gave no sign of it.

In July 1869 An Dehai, at Cixi's secret order, took a trip to the south to purchase cloth and dress material for her. He grabbed the chance to extort money from local officials along his way, causing widespread discontent and indignation. On his arrival in Shandong, he was arrested by the provincial governor, Ding Baozhen. Ding sent a report posthaste to the emperor asking permission to behead An Dehai on the spot.

According to the law of the Qing court eunuchs were strictly forbidden to venture out of the capital, and any trespasser would be punished with death. Empress Dowager Cixi happened to be ill at the time and did not show up for her audience for several days. On receiving Ding's report, Emperor Tongzhi rejoiced at the chance to rid the hated eunuch who had plagued the palace with his presence. Empress Dowager Ci'an showed unusual resolution by ordering An Dehai to be executed without delay. Only after An Dehai's death was Cixi informed of the matter. She burned with rage, but it was too late.

Soon after that, a dispute arose between Cixi and Ci'an over the choice of Emperor Tongzhi's bride. The emperor himself preferred the candidate selected by Ci'an. Thus Cixi suffered yet another defeat in her contention with Ci'an.

After his wedding Emperor Tongzhi was considered to have attained manhood and therefore was ready to rule the empire in his own right. With great reluctance Empress Dowager Cixi relinquished the power to hold court to the emperor and retreated back to the rear palace. However, Emperor Tongzhi remained a nominal ruler, with Cixi manipulating power behind the scenes. After some futile attempts to gain the upper hand over his mother, the emperor gave up the fight and found solace in a dissipated life. He became a frequent visitor to the brothels, where he contracted venereal disease and died as a result.

After Emperor Tongzhi's death Cixi enthroned Emperor Guangxu without consulting Ci'an and resumed the practice of holding court in the emperor's place. As her position became consolidated, she found Ci'an to be an intolerable obstacle to her ambition and plotted to get rid of her. In the meantime, however, her attitude toward Ci'an was most humble and respectful.

On one occasion Ci'an suffered a minor but lingering ailment. Cixi called on her every day to inquire after Ci'an's condition. On one such visit Ci'an noticed that part of Cixi's arm was bandaged in a silk cloth and asked what the matter was. Cixi hastily concealed her arm in her sleeve and tried to change the subject. Ci'an insisted on knowing the cause, and Cixi finally broached her secret with great reluctance, saying that she had put flesh from her own arm into the soup presented the day before. In this way she had hoped to move heaven to grant Ci'an a quick recovery.

The simple-minded Ci'an was moved to tears. "You are so kindhearted, and yet the late emperor did not trust you." She rushed to her bedchamber. On her return she handed a piece of paper to Cixi.

Cixi's hands trembled when she read the paper. It was the secret will left by Emperor Xianfeng, dictating, "If Honored Consort Nala should rely on her son's position and act against law and reason, the empress shall punish her without mercy according the established canons of the imperial clan." It was her knowledge of the existence of such a will that had prevented Cixi from open confrontation with Ci'an. Cixi quickly regained composure and handed the paper back to Ci'an.

Ci'an took it and threw it into the fire. Then she took Cixi by both hands, pledging friendship and expressing a willingness to share responsibilities with her in governing the empire. After an initial surge of gratitude, Cixi was filled with relief and a sense of ultimate triumph.

A few months later Empress Dowager Ci'an suddenly died after, according to one story, eating some cookies sent to her by Cixi. Having rid herself of a long-time rival, Cixi went on to tackle another mortal malady of hers, Yixin.

Yixin had played a vital role in Cixi's successful coup to

eliminate the eight powerful ministers. On account of this, Cixi allowed him to occupy a prominent position in the imperial court. When Cixi began to hold court from behind a curtain, she did not have full control of the situation and lacked experience in attending to various matters of state, so she relied on Yixin out of necessity, but she often tried to remind him of his subordinate status. However, Yixin was not reconciled to her supremacy. He courted the friendship of powerful courtiers to form his own clique, which set Cixi's teeth on edge. In the fourth year of the Tongzhi reign (1865) Yixin, found guilty of some trivial offense, was deprived of all his posts by Cixi. Soon after, however, she arranged for someone to speak in his favor at the court and, in a generous gesture, agreed to reinstate him. This incident made Yixin realize the strength of his opponent, whom he had persistently underestimated. From then on he no longer challenged her authority, but Cixi did not relax her vigilance.

After Emperor Guangxu ascended the throne Cixi's position in the imperial court became impregnable. She no longer had any use for Yixin, whose clout had suffered a drastic decline with the successive deaths of his cohorts at court. Time was ripe for his elimination. But he conducted himself with such circumspection that Cixi could find no excuse to get rid of him.

In the tenth year of the Guangxu reign (1884) the Sino-French war ended with China as the victor. However, the treaty signed after the war contained humiliating terms for China. The whole country was plunged into a furor of indignation, and the court was inundated with denunciations of Yixin, who had negotiated the deal with the French, and angry demands for his dismissal. Though she herself had formulated the policy of capitulation to the French, Cixi shifted the blame on Yixin, depriving him of all his posts and barring him forever from officialdom. At last Cixi had attained absolute supremacy over the Qing court.

At his enthronement Emperor Guangxu was still a baby of only four years age. As he grew older, his intelligence and ambition became more and more apparent to the wary Empress Dowager Cixi. To strengthen her control over the emperor, she forced him to take her niece for his empress. The wedding took place in the fifteenth year of the Guangxu reign (1889). As in the case of Emperor Tongzhi, Cixi relinquished imperial power in favor of Emperor Guangxu and retreated to the rear palace, but again this amounted to a mere gesture.

Influenced by his tutor Weng Tonghe, Emperor Guangxu hoped to revitalize the ancient empire by introducing Western-style reforms, much to the displeasure of Cixi. In the twentieth year of the Guangxu reign (1894) the Sino-Japanese war broke out. With the support of some court ministers, Emperor Guangxu advocated entering the war with full force, hoping thereby to free himself from Cixi's control. Initially Cixi had been ready to fund the war, but when she sensed Emperor Guangxu's intention, she chose to thwart him at the expense of national interests. Because of her intervention, the Qing troops suffered a series of defeats that resulted in the signing of the notorious Maguan Treaty. Emperor Guangxu sent an envoy to Cixi with his message: "Unless the empress dowager hands over imperial power, I will abdicate in favor of someone else and stop ruling the nation in humiliation and disgrace!" Cixi was compelled to promise never to meddle in state affairs again.

In the twenty-fourth year of his reign (1898) Emperor Guangxu issued an edict that started a short-lived reform movement. Reform advocators such as Kang Youwei, Liang Qichao and Tan Sitong were given a chance to bring their ideas into effect. Cixi's response was fast and unequivocal. The following day she had the tutor Weng Tonghe escorted back to his hometown and prohibited him from holding any official position for the rest of his life. Then she issued an edict demanding that all courtiers above the second rank come to her and offer her their thanks, thereby giving them to understand that they owed their position to her and not to the impotent emperor. Her countermeasures proved effective. Emperor Guangxu's call for reform found little response in the empire.

With her trusted follower Rong Lu, Cixi plotted to put the emperor under house arrest. She had a rumor circulated saying that the emperor was terminally ill. Thus the pro-reform officials were kept on tenterhooks.

Emperor Guangxu recognized his perilous position and summoned Liang Qichao and Kang Youwei to a secret meeting, but neither could offer a concrete plan of action. The desperate emperor decided to seek help from Yuan Shikai, a powerful general under Rong Lu's command. Yuan promised to lead his troops to rescue the emperor, but considered it a safer bet to ally with the empress dowager, so he reported the matter to Rong Lu, who hastened to inform Cixi. Infuriated, Cixi had Emperor Guangxu locked up and ordered a hunt for the reformists. She returned to hold court as the supreme ruler of China.

In the twenty-fifth year of the Guangxu reign (1899) the Boxer Movement was launched by the landowners as well as peasants in Shandong, who shared a deep abomination of Western missionaries who they regarded as the cause of all China's troubles. At that time Cixi was fuming over the foreign powers' intervention into the affairs of court. Cashing in on the situation, she declared war against the imperialist powers and rewarded the Boxers for attacking foreigners. In retaliation, the joint forces of the eight imperialist powers (Britain, the United States, Germany, France, Japan, Russia, Austria and Italy) entered in the port city of Tianjin and fought their way into the imperial capital.

Empress Dowager Cixi fled to Xi'an, taking Emperor Guangxu with her. To appease the foreign powers she turned her back on the Boxers and had them suppressed and massacred. In the twenty-seventh year of the Guangxu reign (1901) the Qing government signed yet another humiliating agreement, the Xinchou Treaty, which required China to pay huge war indemnities to the invaders. However, this did not stop Cixi from living in wanton extravagance at the expense of her countrymen.

In the thirty-fourth year of the Guangxu reign (1908) Cixi, then in her seventies, became gravely ill. At this news, Emperor Guangxu, himself a long-time invalid, could hardly contain his excitement, thinking his ordeal would soon be over. When a eunuch informed Cixi of the emperor's reaction, she muttered angrily, "I won't die before him!"

A few days later Emperor Guangxu died. Cixi enthroned three-year-old Puyi, who was to be the last emperor of China. The choice of a baby for the throne clearly indicated her intention of holding onto the power at court, but this time death got the better of her. The following day she breathed her last.

图书在版编目(CIP)数据

中国古代后妃故事：英文/元阳，晓燕编著. —北京：
外文出版社，2001
（中华文明万花筒）
ISBN 7 – 119 – 02041 – 2

Ⅰ.中… Ⅱ.①元… ②晓… Ⅲ.①历史故事 – 中国 – 当代 – 英文
②后妃 – 生平事迹 – 中国 – 古代 – 英文 Ⅳ.I247.8

中国版本图书馆 CIP 数据核字(97)第 05004 号

责任编辑　白雪梅
封面设计　朱振安
插图绘制　李士伋

外文出版社网址：
http://www.flp.com.cn
外文出版社电子信箱：
info@flp.com.cn
sales@flp.com.cn

中国古代后妃故事

元　阳
晓　燕 著

*

ⓒ外文出版社
外文出版社出版
（中国北京百万庄大街 24 号）
邮政编码 100037
通县大中印刷厂印刷
中国国际图书贸易总公司发行
（中国北京车公庄西路 35 号）
北京邮政信箱第 399 号　邮政编码 100044
1998 年(36 开)第 1 版
2001 年第 1 版第 2 次印刷
（英）
ISBN 7 – 119 – 02041 – 2/I·455(外)
03000(平)
10 – E – 3184P